Speaking of Poets

WITHDRAWN

Speaking of Poets

Interviews with Poets Who Write for Children and Young Adults

Written and edited by

Jeffrey S. Copeland
University of Northern Iowa

National Council of Teachers of English
1111 W. Kenyon Road, Urbana, Illinois 61801-1096

Permission acknowledgments appear on page 128.

Manuscript Editor: Julie Riley Bush

Staff Editor: Marlo Welshons

Cover Design: Doug Burnett

Cover Art: © by Susan M. McGinnis

Interior Design: Doug Burnett

NCTE Stock Number: 46228-3050

Library of Congress Cataloging-in-Publication Data

Copeland, Jeffrey Scott, 1953–
    Speaking of poets : interviews with poets who write for children and young adults / written and edited by Jeffrey S. Copeland.
        p.   cm.
    Includes bibliographical references.
    ISBN 0-8141-4622-8
    1. American poetry—20th century—History and criticism—Theory, etc. 2. Young adult poetry, American—History and criticism—Theory, etc. 3. Children's poetry, American—History and criticism—Theory, etc. 4. Poets, American—20th century—Interviews. 5. Young adult poetry—Authorship. 6. Children's poetry—Authorship. I. National Council of Teachers of English. II. Title.
PS325.C7   1993
811'.54099282—dc20   93-22729
                                                                                                      CIP

For my guiding light, my partner,
my love: Vicky Lynn

Contents

Acknowledgments

This project could not have been completed without assistance from many quarters. Thanks and appreciation are in order for the following people:

Michael Spooner for his encouragement, suggestions, and kindness through all stages of the writing;

Vicky and Crystal Lynn Copeland for daily encouragement, help with transcription of interview tapes, computer expertise, and putting up with the clutter, which at times rivaled the mess produced by the Johnstown Flood;

Lucille Lettow, youth librarian supreme, for helping me assemble the many volumes of poetry necessary for this project;

Dee Gaede of B. Dalton Booksellers for helping secure the newest releases in quick order;

Ann and Richard Rupe for providing a wonderful writing studio;

Members of the Children's Literature Assembly for their advice and counsel during the initial stages of the project;

Judith Ayer Doyle of Curbstone Press, Alison Wood of Clarion Books, Kimberly Pfohl of Macmillan Children's Book Group, Laurie Callahan of New Directions Publishing Corporation, and all the other members of publishing firms who helped me acquire photographs of the poets and books in galley form;

Ben Nelms for introducing me to the world of children's poetry and Jerome Klinkowitz for teaching me about the world of publishing;

Marlo Welshons, staff editor, and Julie Riley Bush, manuscript editor, for manuscript preparation and editorial assistance.

Thanks of the highest order is also given to the poets of this volume for sitting through my stacks of questions and for giving so much of themselves to this project. Bless you all.

Introduction

As with the changes in other forms of literature, the poetry written for children and young adults has undergone a steady evolution through the decades. Some of this change has been quite obvious. One merely has to glance through Rachel Field's *Taxis and Toadstools* (1926) and compare it with Arnold Adoff's *Chocolate Dreams* (1989) or Gary Soto's *A Fire in My Hands* (1990) to see such general changes as less attention to rigid poetic forms and formal rhyme scheme and more emphasis given to rhythmic qualities and universal voices within the poems. These and other changes are, of course, important, but the significant evolution in the poetry written for children and young adults has been not so much in the poetry itself but in how the poet views his or her craft and, therefore, the relationship of the poet to the reader. This new intersection of reader and poet is a point of shared experience.

We are now in an era in which poets understand a great deal more about the process of literary response, the process by which the children interact with their poetry. It is an era in which the study of children's poetry preference, a study still in its infancy, has given the poets the power to see within the psyche of the reader. It is an era in which poets speak to their readers not only through the images and ideas in a poem but also through extended notes, dialogues, and comments about how they view the nature of poetry and the wonders of childhood. Poets today invite their young readers to meet them first as people, to read and enjoy their poetry, and then get actively involved physically or symbolically with the printed line. It is a time when Karla Kuskin in *Near the Window Tree: Poems and Notes* (1975) shares with her readers her sources of inspiration for the poems, personal anecdotes related to each, and her philosophy of crafting poetry and then encourages readers to write their own. At the same time, Gary Soto in *A Fire in My Hands* not only provides detailed introductions for his poems but also describes his own personal process of composing in a "Question and Answer" section at the end of the book. It is a time when Myra Cohn Livingston introduces a young speaker in "I Havent Learned to Whistle," (from *O Sliver of Liver and Other Poems,* 1979) and readers everywhere pucker their lips. It is a time when reader and poet come together and build a common ground of understanding.

This project was begun as a means of continuing and illuminating this shared experience among the poets, readers, teachers, librarians, and others who share poetry with young readers. I asked leaders of the Children's Literature Assembly of the National Council of Teachers of English to identify poets they would most like to have presented for examination. They also offered suggestions related to the format of the book. The interview format was chosen for this project in order to keep the poets' responses as candid, natural, and informal as possible. This would allow the poets an opportunity to present and give emphasis to areas of their own lives and works they wished to share.

I also decided that even though there was a small group of questions that the assembly wanted every poet to respond to, a standard list would not be used for all. Rather, other interview questions would be designed based upon the specific works and unique experiences of each poet.

This project took me from an overstuffed couch in front of a crackling fire in Barbara Juster Esbensen's den in Edina, Minnesota, to the family room/library/museum of Arnold Adoff's magnificent homestead in Yellow Springs, Ohio. However, not all interviews could be conducted in such settings. Some of the poets travel across the country to share their poetry so frequently that their homes proved little more than pit stops; interviews with these poets, of necessity, were conducted by telephone. The only out-of-the-ordinary "interview" was conducted with Lilian Moore. This turned out to be a mail interview, with questions and responses traveling thousands of miles before the final format was achieved.

Looking back now upon the interviews, several common ideas and elements appeared from poet to poet. First, with few exceptions, the poets described their childhoods as being vivid, wonderful times. They continue to draw upon these experiences in their own writings and encourage young readers to make the most of this special time in life. Aileen Fisher went so far as to say children should be held out of school for a few extra years to allow them more time just to be kids. The poets, to a person, also believed that poems should appear as puzzles and be full of surprises for younger readers. In order for this to occur, X. J. Kennedy, Myra Cohn Livingston, and Eve Merriam suggested that poems be read aloud, read aloud, and read aloud again.

It also became clear that these individuals are some of the most well-traveled people in the country. From Jimmy Santiago Baca to Lee Bennett Hopkins, the poets travel from school to school while sharing their lives and works with their readers. At these sessions, they present writing as a process, one requiring much care and diligence. Arnold

Adoff shares his "scrolls" to emphasize stages in the revision process; Barbara Juster Esbensen shows mounds of papers that house draft after draft of her poems. The lone exception is Aileen Fisher, who prefers to write and stay at home on the outskirts of Boulder, Colorado.

Most poets described themselves as "pack rats," each keeping all around their homes scraps of paper containing images, fragments of poems, or interesting lines. X. J. Kennedy, Mel Glenn, and Karla Kuskin, in particular, said that major disasters would occur if anyone ever entered their homes and cleaned up these storehouses of information. William Cole, in addition to his notes, has nearly four thousand volumes of poetry lining his walls. All were quite proud of the clutter.

In terms of the process of composing the poems, the poets called writing a detailed process of revision. Gary Soto mentioned that he hated the actual writing; what he enjoyed was the revising and completion of writing tasks. Karla Kuskin said she wasn't a writer at all; she described herself as a "rewriter." Eve Merriam described revision as a "cleansing act." Arnold Adoff will do as many as seventy-five drafts/revisions for a single poem; Valerie Worth likewise has done hundreds of drafts for one "small poem." Eloise Greenfield loves to revise in the quiet hours after midnight. All mentioned the revision process was a true joy for them.

On the other side, differences could also be seen among the poets. Many have written books and other pieces about teaching and sharing poetry with the young, and in the end all believe that poetry should be exciting, should be fun, should be a magical experience for young readers. However, means to this end are quite varied. Myra Cohn Livingston believes knowledge about the craft of poetry and poetic forms is essential to achieving enjoyment and success in writing. Barbara Juster Esbensen shares her unique method of weaving images and calls for careful observation on the part of the reader. Gary Soto suggests that young readers spend their time gathering "working life" experiences and suggests that they do no serious writing until they are in their twenties. The means may differ, but all are striving for an enriched intersection of reader and print.

The poets' writing careers were also shaped by a variety of other poets: Eve Merriam actually studied with W. H. Auden and cherished the work of Gerard Manley Hopkins. Gary Soto was influenced most by the works of Lawrence Ferlinghetti and Pablo Neruda. Barbara Juster Esbensen listed both Amy Lowell and Sara Teasdale as having a great influence upon the development of form in her poetry. Arnold Adoff said e. e. cummings did *not* influence his style, a fact that will surprise many.

Finally, after talking with the poets, a conclusion was simple enough: The poetry being written for children and young adults is in good hands. While all share many similarities in areas ranging from philosophies to structures, they appear as so many fingerprints scattered across a well-used door. Each has a trademark, a locus of control. Each provides for children an invitation to the magnificent world of poetry. Each shares a love of poetry, a love of children, a love of life. Each unlocks the special gifts only poetry can provide.

Arnold Adoff

Arnold Adoff is a writer on a mission. For the past twenty-five years, Adoff has been influencing how young readers view such matters as equality of races, sex-role stereotyping, individual rights, and ageism. A deeply compassionate man, Adoff has spent his writing career expounding the strength of family, both in terms of the individual family structure and the family of humanity.

Arnold Adoff began his writing career as an anthologist. His anthologies, which were born of necessity to supplement his own teaching, presented an array of outstanding African American writers for students who for too long had not found such material available in the schools. I Am the Darker Brother *(1968) and* City in All Directions *(1969), both award-winning anthologies, are considered ground-breaking books in the field of literature for children and young adults.*

Readers young and old are delighted by the range of subjects covered by Arnold Adoff, from the world of the fantastic in The Cabbages Are Chasing the Rabbits *(1985) to the poet's prose of* Flamboyan *(1988). His wish is always to be considered controversial, to make readers juggle emotions and reconsider deeply rooted beliefs as they examine his poetry. In 1988 Adoff received the National Council of Teachers of English Award for Excellence in Poetry for Children. Today, he lives and creates with his wife, Virginia Hamilton, in Yellow Springs, Ohio.*

JC: Many times you have said that you first started writing for children because you wanted to play a small part in changing the beliefs and attitudes of society; you wanted to help young readers see and feel a true multiethnic, multicultural world.

AA: It is certainly difficult to publish poetry in America. It's difficult to "become" a poet. I was first a teacher using African American poetry, what then was called Negro poetry, with my students who were white, black, and from various Hispanic cultures. To go from a classroom in Harlem with material that you have collected for classroom use to making a book was a major breakthrough. To be a white anthologist whose first work was a collection of black poetry was very difficult and very special to me. After several years of making an impact that way, to begin to publish my own poetry was perhaps even more

Photo: Virginia Hamilton Adoff

difficult, because people, especially those in publishing, put a single label on you. You are a teacher, not a poet. Or you're an anthologist, not a poet. But those are personal kinds of goals and achievements. In terms of the work itself, I have continued to present perspectives, visions, and voices from other cultures outside of the mainstream. I'm married to Virginia Hamilton, so we live the ultimate integrationist life in this family. We have two biracial children. So, the work I have done all these years has been for my own children as well as for the children and teenagers I have taught in New York. More than that, the work I do attempts to present the real America to young people, because politically I could not create any other way. If one element of society is excluded or made secondary, then the whole of America falls like a house of cards. Then there is no hope for the future in the country. All that goes beyond race; that goes to gender as well, as in *Flamboyan* or some of the other books I have done with "little girl" voices. The work also goes to generations, as in a book like *Hard to Be Six* (1991). That's really what it is all about. It is personal and it is political. It has to do with my people and other peoples as well.

JC: Have you considered moving ahead from something like *Black Is Brown Is Tan* (1973) to more of a Latin with East Asian with Native American with *everyone* flavor in your work? Why not even more space in your work showing all different types of folks living together and becoming one?

AA: I have under contract a new book that will be the first collection/anthology that I have done since 1975 when I gave up working on anthologies to concentrate on publishing my own poetry. This collection will be called *The Next America* and will be the voices of many peoples in America. My wife, Virginia, has coined a phrase: *parallel cultures.* This view takes you away from majority/minority thinking. If you look at parallel cultures in America, particularly with great immigration influxes, you see culture after culture, not a melting pot. You see people living side by side, hopefully interacting and treating each other equally. The struggle is to make that a reality. It is also a struggle to bring those voices into children's literature. At present I am also working with several others to form a multicultural committee. This committee, which will be set up in New York, will foster and encourage work coming in from a variety of people.

For me, working on *The Next America* has been a natural outgrowth of the anthologies I designed earlier. As I mentioned, I stopped doing anthologies because I wanted to establish myself as a poet. In addition to that, by the mid- and late-1970s two things were happening in America. One, there were other writers, particularly black writers, who were doing more and more work in children's literature, and they were presenting their own voices. Enough of a body of African American literature had been published and established that I achieved some of my goals. Also, I began to feel that each group should take control of presenting their own voices. I have always maintained that as much in tune as I am in my life, I'm still not a person of color, living every day that way, or writing from that perspective. The other thing that happened was it became very, very difficult in the 1970s and 1980s to create a multicultural work. The most difficult times I have had in getting books published have been with books that have been of mixed message. America today can deal with side-by-side and certainly with tokenism and certainly here and there with integration, but a collection like *City in All Directions* has a hard time getting published. By no means is the effort over. Only a small percentage of the superb African American poetry has been published. There has been no collection of contemporary Native American poetry published. There is a long way to go in terms of children's literature and literature for older readers in this area of presenting the individual groups and their poetry, let alone prose. That is why I am attempting to put them all side by side in this new *The Next America* collection and in all of my other work.

JC: Tell us about Arnold Adoff the writer. How would you describe your own process of composing?

AA: I'm a slow writer. I'm a writer whose life is filled with other things. I'm very much involved with family, traveling, speaking at functions and workshops, and working with young people. I am always distracted. Fortunately, I work in short forms, and I can go back and forth between art and life, writing and living, even in the course of the same day. I'm the agent in the family, so I do all the business side. I attempt to overcome living and creating in the midst of chaos by working slowly and steadily. I attempt to set up schedules, which I am always breaking. I try to devote several hours a day to the business side, then I turn all attention to the writing.

I am very much a believer in rewriting; writing is rather a small part of what I do. The heat, the excitement, and the joy of scribbling is the writing, and that is only the very beginning of the process. I can do as many as seventy-five drafts of a single poem. Typical for me is nineteen or twenty drafts. As I travel around the country and work with children, I take my scrolls with me. I keep my drafts, from the rough sketches on, on these scrolls. I tape them together or use long rolls of paper or computer paper. Because I work on short pieces, all of this rewriting and draft after draft will end up as a poem that usually is on a single page. That is a key element to me. I believe in the short piece. The shorter the piece, the more difficult the piece, and the greater the challenge. The shorter the piece, the more the elements of inference and implication enter into things. I try to write as short as possible to satisfy my own artistic aesthetic, and I write as short as possible because that is the most exciting presentation that can be given to a young reader.

For those who are interested in reading my poetry, I say they have to read each poem at least three times. The first time should be to get the meaning, the semantic line of force of my work. Everyone who writes for communication has a semantic line of force: Something means something. You first read a poem, whether it is Adoff or Shakespeare or anything in between, for what it has to say. Second, my work has to be read for how it sings. In all of my work, even in the poet's prose of *Flamboyan,* there are musical or rhythmic elements that must be enjoyed by the reader. My work should then be read a third time for structure. The shaping and the forming is very deliberate. A great deal of the revision process happens because I am saying and singing at the same time. That is complex enough, but in draft after draft I'm reshaping my work for all of the flush rights, flush lefts, and spaces between letters, the line spaces between lines, and stanzation. All of this is very important. This is why my theory is that a reader has to go back to a poem more than one time to understand precisely what is involved and catch implication and inference. I don't write for adults or young people who are not willing to commit the effort. If I'm true to what I believe, then as I shape and form my poems I create a structure that pulls the eye and, of course, the brain follows. Each eye movement is a millisecond of time, and time is rhythm, and rhythm is the music that is in my writing. This is something that is very important to me; otherwise, I would be a prose writer.

My definition of poetry is that it is "shaped speech." It has to be colloquial, it has to be relevant, it has to be exciting, and it has to be short. So much is left out that the reader, younger or older, has to bring the richness of past experience to the poem. I shape and form to pull the eye along from the first letter of the first word. That even has to do with punctuation and use of upper- and lowercase letters. In some books every word begins with a capital letter and there is no punctuation; in some works I use no capitalization and punctuation; in some books

I have upper- and lowercase and "normal" punctuation. I do this because punctuation and capitalization also affect the rhythm and movement just like a stop sign affects our driving. I do so many drafts because I'm attempting to create a work that has a structure that will reveal itself to the reader. Hopefully, if I've done my job well, it will— even with only one reading.

JC: In terms of stylistic matters, what were the early influences on you as a writer?

AA: Sometimes in my earlier work people would see that I worked in lowercase and they would say, "e. e. cummings." Nothing could have been further from the truth. Those who are interested in what I do need to go back to French imagists and some of the constructivist painters and sculptors of the early 1900s. I'm probably more influenced by skyscrapers and great city piles of brick and steel than I am by poets creating in the halcyon days of the 1920s as cummings did. My work is personal, but I mean to communicate to the youngest child. More and more, particularly in this time of whole-language and literature-based curricula, I see a great many books of mine used in kindergarten and first grade when I thought the readers would be those who are nine, ten, twelve years old. That, I think, says something great about teachers who are getting into poetry, because they realize the great values that are there for shaping critical thinking.

JC: Encircling all in *In for Winter, Out for Spring* (1991) is a strong sense of family and the security that belonging to a family provides. This "family time" is a dominant theme running through your work.

AA: Family is all I know. I use family in the sense of structure. In many ways, I have a fragmented family on both sides. My father was born in Europe and came to America in 1912 when he was twelve. I have lost touch with a great many family relatives and with the whole of the family in Europe. My wife's grandfather was born into slavery and came to Yellow Springs, Ohio, as a very young boy. Other than an Alex Haley making a leap through history, as an African American one can only go back just so far in tracing roots. So, whether my works are illustrated as all white, or interracial, or all black, and whatever the perspectives, whether it be the seasons or hugging and kissing or whatever the activity, family is the structure. That is the strength element I chose to present to kids. I have done so in many kinds of books: the family in *Tornado!* (1977), the African family in *Ma nDA LA* (1971), the family in *Black Is Brown Is Tan*. Sometimes I have role reversals. *Black*

Is Brown Is Tan was published twenty years ago, and I have the father cooking and the mother chopping wood. All these things are done on purpose. Everything is done consciously.

JC: In *Sports Pages* (1986), one comes to another characteristic of your work: Instead of using a "neutral" speaker for the poems, you chose to make it quite clear the speaker of many poems is a "she."

AA: I create kids and the voices of kids. If I'm writing for children, I'm not going to be an adult writing down to kids in a condescending way, but I'm not going to attempt to have an adult voice speaking to young people. I think I'm arrogant enough from my years on this planet to continue to create young voices to speak directly to young readers and to adults. That frees me to become a young girl in *I Am the Running Girl* (1979). It also frees me to become a bird in other pieces or even be an androgynous voice in *Friend Dog* (1980) where you really don't know if it is a boy or a girl. Occasionally, as in *Big Sister Tells Me That I'm Black* (1976), it frees me to go outside my race.

I deal with flesh and blood. I try to create real kids and say real things for real readers. Also, I am trying to create change in the heads of kids. To put it very simply, when I speak with kids I say, "I want to move you from Point A to Point B. If you just stay at Point A, then maybe I have entertained you and maybe it has been fun. If I can move you from Point A to Point B, then you can see something important." And I mean this not just in race or gender but maybe in something ordinary that is often overlooked. The young reader may see something differently for the first time. That is a large part of what I do.

JC: The Cabbages Are Chasing the Rabbits is a very different sort of collection for you. The fantasy, the role reversals of creatures, the repetition of a common line in several poems—all are quite different from what one would expect from you.

AA: Some of my books are collections, like *Greens* (1989) and *Eats* (1979) and *Chocolate Dreams* (1989). And some of my books are very subversive stylistically as well as in other ways, because they are collections of individual poems that do prose work. A book like *I Am the Running Girl* is a single story. A book like *The Cabbages Are Chasing the Rabbits* is a single story. These are done through a series of interconnecting poems. *Cabbages* is different because it is a whole piece of music. I have a scroll where I have taken the pages before they were bound and have marked them in the same way we mark pieces of music. The symmetry in that book is absolutely precise, and not just in section by section. If you examine it page by page, line by line, phrase by phrase, almost to the letter the music is precisely symmetrical, whether it be when the cabbages are chasing the rabbits, the rabbits chasing the dogs, the dogs the hunters. That was a very difficult book to do to satisfy myself personally, because I wanted to work in a symmetrical, musical form. Symmetry is an important element in all of my work and in this book particularly. Then, I wanted to do the role reversal to turn reality upside-down, because I think that makes for a great deal of fresh vision and insight into the world. It worked out that I was doing a very nice antihunting poem, which I didn't realize at the time. I have had quite a few angry letters from hunters over this one!

JC: Tell us about your visits to the schools to work with young readers.

AA: Several times each fall I kick off a big festival in a school or school district. I go in for a few days and come back in the spring for the big celebration. I always show my scrolls and attempt to get teachers and kids to work in a more vertical fashion through keeping track of their revisions, rather than having folders of individual sheets of paper, which I call horizontal working. I try to set up classrooms where every kid has a scroll hanging on the wall, and when they come in the room they take these down and write and rewrite and critique each other. I also like intergrade critiquing, where older and younger kids send materials back and forth. I spend a lot of time talking about researching, digging up facts, and making your work realistic in fact and in fantasy elements. I'm a great believer that the fantasy has to be just as realistic as the reality. My fantasy is as detailed and realistic as the reality, and I think that that is something that separates me from many writers. I talk about all of this with children.

JC: Many consider your poetry—especially in terms of the themes and subjects you cover, your use of poet's prose, your own particular use of punctuation—to be very different from the mainstream of contemporary poetry being written for children and young adults. How do you see your work as being different?

AA: First of all, I may be innovative, but my work should not be described as experimental. I do things that are idiosyncratic in terms of my own aesthetic. All of the materials I use when I create my literature come from "adult poetry." So little poetry is published for children. Much of what is published is verse. So much has been in the model of the Edward Lear and Robert Louis Stevenson Eurocentric, British and British-American model. Compared to that, my work looks tremendously out of place to some people and difficult for them to adjust to, even though I have been publishing for almost twenty-five years. But if you have taken a look at what has happened in post-World War II American adult poetry, then I am just one of hundreds and hundreds of poets who have taken many of these literary tools and materials from influences all over the world. In that context, I may seem out of place in literature for children.

I'm still attempting to influence kids in one way or another, whether it is the way they view the color of skin or reality and fantasy. I hope always to be considered perhaps controversial, perhaps dangerous, to the status quo. The artist's job is not to work within the rules to be easily understood by those who attempt to become the taste-makers. It is a struggle to get any poetry published, but it's also a struggle to create something you hope is art. I work long and hard at my craft. I like to feel I have good instincts when it comes to language. All in all, I am very proud of what I have done.

Select Bibliography

Hard to Be Six (Lothrop, 1991).

In for Winter, Out for Spring (Harcourt Brace Jovanovich, 1991).

Chocolate Dreams (Lothrop, 1989).

Greens: Poems (Lothrop, 1989).

Flamboyan (Harcourt Brace Jovanovich, 1988).

Sports Pages (J. B. Lippincott, 1986).

The Cabbages Are Chasing the Rabbits (Harcourt Brace Jovanovich, 1985).

All the Colors of the Race (Lothrop, 1982).

OUTside INside Poems (Lothrop, 1981).

Today We Are Brother and Sister (Lothrop, 1981).

Friend Dog (J. B. Lippincott, 1980).

Eats: Poems (Lothrop, 1979).

I Am the Running Girl (Harper & Row, 1979).

under the early morning trees (E. P. Dutton, 1978).

Tornado! (Delacorte, 1977).

Big Sister Tells Me That I'm Black (Holt, 1976).

make a circle, keep us in (Delacorte, 1975).

Black Is Brown Is Tan (Harper & Row, 1973).
Ma nDA LA (Harper & Row, 1971).

Anthologies Edited

Celebrations (Follett, 1977).
My Black Me (E. P. Dutton, 1974).
The Poetry of Black America (Harper & Row, 1973).
it is the poem singing into your eyes (Harper & Row, 1971).
Black Out Loud (Macmillan, 1969).
City in All Directions (Macmillan, 1969).
I Am the Darker Brother (Macmillan, 1968).

Lilian Moore

Lilian Moore would like to see poetry become an everyday part of growing up. In particular, she suggests that in the schools poetry be shared in all subject areas and in all possible manners in order for children to see its full range and beauty. She believes that when children are introduced to this spectrum of poetry, they should be given not only rhymes and jingles but also poems that touch feelings and offer food for thought.

Lilian Moore's poetry is characterized by simplicity of style, powerful imagery, and humor. Subjects for her poems range from the world of nature, as in Sam's Place: Poems from the Country *(1973), to the world of the supernatural, as in* See My Lovely Poison Ivy, and Other Verses about Witches, Ghosts, and Things *(1975). Moore captures universal experiences of childhood in these poems: listening to the soft sounds of the rain, pretending to be asleep late at night, being awed by the sights of the city.*

Lilian Moore received the National Council of Teachers of English Award for Excellence in Poetry for Children in 1985. She lives today in Kerhonkson, New York.

Photo: Joan Glazer

JC: You have long been concerned about getting poetry and children together. Please share your ideas about the natural connection between young children and poetry.

LM: Children start out looking at the world very much as poets do—as if everything were new, as indeed it is to the young child. They are adventuresome with language in the same spirit poets are: taking pleasure in rhyme, in playfulness with words, in unexpected word happenings. The language of young children often has the expressiveness and directness of poetry.

Young children often think as poets do—in metaphor, one of the building blocks of poetry, a fresh and vivid way of looking at the world. It's Shakespeare saying, "Juliet is the sun." It's Picasso changing modern sculpture through metaphor: taking a bicycle saddle and handlebars and creating the head of a bull.

The poet Judith Thurman looked at a black fire escape in the white sun and saw "morning grazing like a zebra" outside a window. One day I saw a small child shine a new flashlight on the ceiling and cry, "Hello, sun!" The poet Valerie Worth speaks of a turtle "shawled in the shade of his shell." I heard a child seeing her first turtle say excitedly, "Look at the bonnet that he wears!"

We miss a lot when we dismiss children's imagery as just cute. It is funny, of course, to see a young child watching his mother sipping a drink through a straw and then saying, "I want a noodle, too!" But the child is connecting experience effectively.

If we all spoke one language I think we would find some universal aspect to the imagery of young children. In 1963, the University of California published a book called *From Two to Five* by the Russian poet and translator Kornei Chikovsky. Chikovsky was not only an eminent scholar of adult literature, but he was also a poet of childhood beloved by the children of what was then the Soviet Union. For over fifty years he collected the observations that little children made about life and death and everything in between. People all over that vast land would send him the comments of children. The book *From Two to Five* brought us a small portion of his work. I found this book so full of the enchanting perceptions of children that once when I was in the Soviet Union I asked some people in children's publishing if I could meet Kornei Chikovsky. He was eighty-five at the time, a tall, marvelous-looking man with a mane of white hair and a passionate interest in children and poetry. In the course of our conversation I told him that when my son was little and first saw the half-moon, he cried out, "Look! The moon is broke!" Chikovsky jumped up from his chair and said eagerly, "I must write that down!" I had this wonderful moment when I could say to him, "You don't have to. In your book *From Two to Five* you tell of a Russian child who said the very same thing."

JC: You have said that children who have poems in their lives are lucky. Would you comment on that?

LM: All too often as children grow older their spontaneity—their ability to see the world afresh—goes underground like a stream that leaves only the dry riverbed. Poems in the life of a child can be like the dowsing sticks that are said to find underground streams. They help children to stay in touch with their own imaginations. And because poems are more than just an arrangement of words, they help children to grow in all the ways that poets offer them: in the power to connect with the feelings of others, to hear the music of their own language, to see the details in the world around them more vividly, more truthfully.

JC: What suggestions have you for those who work with young children? How can they make poetry part of the lives of these youngsters?

LM: What would it be like if poems were an everyday part of growing up? If that underground stream were constantly primed and replenished? What if there were lots of poems in the lives of children, consumed as matter-of-factly as vitamins? What if poetry didn't wear Sunday clothes but jeans and sneakers? And since adults are the bringers of poems to children, wouldn't it be nice if adults were more comfortable with poetry? So many aren't.

JC: Why do you think this is so?

LM: I think partly it's because we grew up thinking there have to be right answers all the time. So we look for right answers to poems. But poems deal with feelings and perceptions. The poet wants to share an experience, something that has been seen or felt or pondered. The poet takes it for granted that different people will respond differently to the poems, perhaps find their own answers. Think of that famous and beautiful poem by Robert Frost, "Stopping by Woods on a Snowy Evening." Those magical last lines! The poem is so carefully crafted that the poet simply had to add that extra last line about miles to go before sleeping. And when he did it went off like a rocket in the imaginations of people.

Hundreds of people asked Robert Frost what it meant, searching perhaps for a "right" answer. And he often replied with a joke. Once he said simply, "It was getting dark and I wanted to go home." But of course the poem came from very deep feelings. And like a stone dropped into a lake it has set off ripples that go on to distant shores in people's minds.

Children have highly sensitized antennae in this pursuit of the "right" answer. John Holt wrote an excellent book called *How Children Fail,* in which he demonstrates how carefully children watch the face of the teacher who's asking the question to see if they are getting warmer, closer to the right answer. When we first started the Arrow Book Club at Scholastic, I used to talk to children in many cities about the books they especially wanted. I remember being with a group of youngsters in the library, asking what kind of books they would like us to choose for them. It was clear they were trying to corral the "right" answer. One child virtuously asked for "a geography book," another for a school history book. I said, looking puzzled, "You mean you can have any kind of book you want and you want us to give you a history or geography book?" They caught on soon that there wasn't a "right" answer, and then, as if they had been liberated, they began talking about what they really wanted.

JC: Then how can we, as you say, make poetry an "everyday part of growing up" for children?

LM: What if poetry were, for young children particularly, just an unstructured everyday happening? I know, for one, how happy I would be if I knew that a kindergarten teacher who is about to take her class out to recess on a frosty day would say, as they were putting on their mittens, "Here's something you can do today..."

> Breathe and blow
> White clouds
>   with every puff.
> It's cold today,
>   cold enough
> to see your breath.
> Huff!
> Breathe dragon smoke
>   today!
>
> ("Dragon Smoke," from *I Feel the Same Way,* 1967)

Perhaps they would all blow "dragon smoke" as I so loved to do in my childhood.

Here is another fantasy: It's a spring thaw in the city or the suburbs. A group of middle graders troop into the classroom or perhaps the library. Amid the smell of wet wool and damp boots, the teacher says, "You think it's wet here today. Here is what a poet who lives in the country calls 'wet' ":

> Wet wet wet
> the world of melting winter,
> icicles weeping themselves away
> on the eaves
> little brown rivers streaming
> down the road
> nibbling
> at the edges of the tired snow,
>   all puddled mud
>   not a dry place to put
>   a booted foot,
> everything
>   dripping
>   gushing

    slushing
    slipping
and listen to that brook,
    rushing
like a puppy loosed from its leash.

("Wet," from *Sam's Place: Poems from the Country*)

It was a deeply satisfying experience to walk one day into a classroom in which the children were waiting to see whether a moth or butterfly would eventually emerge from a cocoon in their science corner. It was like a make-a-poet-happy day! Hanging comfortably near the cocoon, as if among friends, was a chart with my poem:

Don't shake this
bough
Don't try
to wake me
now.
In this cocoon
I've work to
do.
Inside this silk
I'm changing
things.

I'm worm-like now
but in this
dark
I'm growing wings.

("Message from a Caterpillar," from *Little Raccoon and Poems from the Woods*, 1975)

Another occasion on which I was glad I wrote poems for children was a visit to a class that had been studying the turning of the year. They all knew about equinoxes, when days and nights are equal, and they all were familiar with the solstices. They knew June 21 was the longest day of the year, and they were especially intrigued that after December 21, the shortest day of the year, the days would imperceptibly lengthen toward spring. It moved me greatly when the teacher read my poem "December 21" (from *Something New Begins*, 1982)—when "temperatures bleed to zero/ but something new begins." What was so especially satisfying in these experiences was the natural way the poems were used—not as some formal curriculum-mandated material but as a way of including an emotional commentary.

JC: How do you think the special language of poetry affects children?

LM: The gift that poetry keeps on giving to children is the gift of their own language. We live in a time of great inarticulateness, when even President Bush speaks of a "vision thing." On T.V. we hear the sports commentator say, "Let's reminisce about the game tomorrow." We breathe in language pollution, lots of it, every day. When children hear poetry, it's as if they are getting deep draughts of language oxygen.

I have an eight-year-old friend who spent the summer nearby. This last Labor Day, she came to say good-bye. Her family was moving back to the city where she goes to school. I asked her how she felt about leaving the country. "Well," she replied, "I am going to be in the third grade, and that's exciting, you know." Then she sighed, "But I hate to leave here." I told her I had a gift for her. "I'm going to give you a word," I said, "that tells you how you feel. The word is 'ambivalent.'" She seemed to taste the word and like it. Later I received a postcard that said, "Thank you for the word 'ambivalent.' I used it the first day of school!"

Even a word can be a gift.

JC: Think about the great range of poetry available today for young readers. How would you suggest that those who work with children help them develop a taste for good poetry?

LM: When we first set up the Arrow Book Club program, we offered a smorgasbord of titles which included junk food. It was out of hope that the child who started out reading only a joke book would move to real reading encouraged by the array of good, varied titles we made available.

There is, of course, junk food in the world of children's poetry. It has its place—verse to amuse or relax. But if we want children's taste to develop, the smorgasbord of poems that we offer must include nutritious fare. Rhymes and jingles may serve a good purpose, but one hopes there will be real poems—poems with muscle, poems that touch feelings, poems that offer ideas and language. Fortunately, it is easier than ever before to make good poems part of a child's life. Many fine poets have been writing for children for some time now. There are anthologies of every kind to browse through. It is even more interesting to go to the work of a single poet. Adults and children may have a surprisingly good time getting to know the voice of an individual poet. Something wonderful may happen, too. They may find poems they love. Those are the best kind to share. When that happens my counsel is:

Go with the poem.

Hang glide
above new landscape
into other weather.

Sail the poem.
Lift.
Drift over treetops
and towers.

Loop with the poem.
Swoop, dip.
Land.
Where?
Trust the poem

("Go with the Poem," from *Go with the Poem*, 1979)

Select Bibliography

I'll Meet You at the Cucumbers (Macmillan, 1988).

Something New Begins (Atheneum, 1982).

Think of Shadows (Atheneum, 1980).

Little Raccoon and Poems from the Woods (McGraw Hill, 1975).

See My Lovely Poison Ivy, and Other Verses about Witches, Ghosts, and Things (Atheneum, 1975).

Sam's Place: Poems from the Country (Atheneum, 1973).

Spooky Rhymes and Riddles (Scholastic, 1973).

I Thought I Heard the City (Atheneum, 1969).

I Feel the Same Way (Atheneum, 1967).

Anthologies Edited

Go with the Poem (McGraw Hill, 1979).

Mel Glenn

Mel Glenn's poetry is the poetry of introspection. Perhaps more so than any other contemporary poet, Glenn expresses the hopes, fears, tears, loves, and disasters of young adults. Subjects for his poems range from the divorce of parents to the loss of a friend to the first pangs of love to life after graduation. The world found within this poetry is sometimes not happy; it is a world full of uncertainty, full of change, full of shadows. The speakers in this world walk a tight line between hope and despair.

Mel Glenn's poetry is characterized by attention to detail and startling comparisons. A poem about watching the violence of soap operas shifts to the reality of a house being robbed. A poem about emigrating to America becomes a walk down the aisle at graduation. All are told in free verse, which allows the natural voice patterns of the speakers to carry the lines.

Mel Glenn, a high school English instructor, draws many characters from his students and colleagues. These characters may originate in Glenn's private world, but they are universal. They are characters young adults know and understand.

Mel Glenn resides in Brooklyn, New York.

JC: Please share with us some background related to your early life and development as a writer.

MG: First of all, my father was a writer. He wrote for a Yiddish paper here in New York. He was a doctor, so he wrote a medical column for this paper. He also wrote a book about diabetes and was really a biblical scholar. Partly because of this, I really think there is a little gene on my chromosome that says, "Write, write, write!" My influences were environmental and also hereditary. And I think both of these were the earliest influences on my writing. Thinking about it now, I can remember helping my father with his articles. He wrote in three or four languages, not that I knew them, but when he wrote in English I helped him with the text of the articles. This was my first real writing experience. I really believe that some people are born to play music and some are born to paint. I wouldn't go so

Photo: Clarion Books

far as to say there is a genetic factor to write, but maybe a genetic predisposition exists for some people. I'd say there was for me.

JC: And growing from these experiences, what were your first pieces to be published?

MG: When I was younger, there was little I thought I could do, but I knew I could write. I went to college at New York University, and I worked four years for the newspaper there. I started as a sports reporter. I covered games at the old Garden when NYU would play basketball there and later developed a feature column, which I loved. People would see my pieces and say, "Oh, you wrote that!" Once, a professor read one of my columns, a satiric column, in class, and I said, "Hey, I like this. I can do this!" I thought that when I finished college I would somehow go into journalism.

But Sargent Shriver, who was the head of the Peace Corps then, came to NYU, and I had to interview him. As part of the story I filled out the application for the Peace Corps. The form said, "Where do you wish to be stationed?" I wrote down "Africa" in that space and sent it off. I really believe in divine intervention, because I was looking through graduate school catalogs and decided that I didn't want to go to school. Then an invitation came for training for the Peace Corps, because of that form I had completed. I went to Indiana, and spent the summer in Bloomington and Terre Haute; then I went overseas to Sierra Leone, West Africa. I kept a diary as I traveled throughout Africa. In fact, I left Nigeria three days before the first revolution. I guess you could say I was one of President Kennedy's children.

I wrote a lot in college, and I wrote a few articles while overseas. Then, I came back to the United States, and now I am a teacher who moonlights as a writer.

JC: How much has the teaching aspect of your career influenced your work as a writer?

MG: The experiences are inseparable. I'm a writer because I am a teacher. If I weren't a teacher, I couldn't get near the stories I write about. I teach now in the same high school I attended. I get very close to the kids. Recently, I was a dean, which in New York is like a counselor. I heard the stories of these kids, their public faces and their private torments. This got me thinking about writing, and it was just a matter of finding the right form for it. Writing is a gift, but you have to be lucky, too. I've been very lucky. One of the things in teaching that's important to me is that every kid is a gift, and every kid has a story. It's these stories I focus on in my writing.

I can give an exact date for my beginning as a writer for young people: January 1, 1980. It was a New Year's resolution of mine. Another teacher in school had shown me a manuscript, and I thought it was horrible. I said to my wife, "I could do better." And she said, "Oh, yeah?" So, January 1, 1980, I wrote my first poem. And I made myself a promise that every day I would write at least one poem. Then a book grew and grew until finally I had enough for *Class Dismissed* (1982). It's very unusual for writers to be able to pinpoint when they started their first book, but I can!

JC: Please expand upon this and tell us about your work habits as a writer. You started by writing one poem a day. How have you evolved since those days?

MG: I have the technological IQ of a carrot. My kids laugh at me because I have trouble programming a VCR. When I write, and especially when I write poetry because there is a lot of crossing out, I write in pencil. I use a Sharpwriter pencil. I finally broke down recently and purchased a very simple word processor. But basically, I write longhand. Then if I like it, I write it again on the machine. When I write a poem over again, it sort of edits itself. It's a natural selection process.

I teach and I have a full day. With the poetry I had to make special time to write, whether it was on the weekends or one o'clock in the morning. I wait until I hear a good story or an idea hits me. I once read that writing is like an open window. Sometimes the thoughts flow and everything just breezes, and sometimes no matter what you do you don't get word one on the page. So, you walk away and come back later. I have plenty of papers to grade and lessons to make when I come home from school. So, I really have to find and make this special time to write. However, when I do write, the clock ceases to exist. I just go on a streak.

JC: In *Class Dismissed*, many subjects are harsh, stark—about parents preparing for divorce, a teen being thrown out of the house, being alone, being afraid of living, being beaten by a parent. This is not the usual fare in contemporary poetry for children and young adults.

MG: These are hard times, not only economically but emotionally for kids. As kids go through life there is a private side that they don't always talk about. And kids tend to look at things seriously. They go through life majoring in theater. *Everything* is a crisis. I had a girl today in my class whose former boyfriend was harassing her, coming to her house to bother her. These kids, in New York especially, lead serious lives. In many ways it is a hard life for them. Some of these kids come from very troubled neighborhoods. I once read that 60 percent of all kids in New York come from one-parent homes, which makes their schooling even more difficult. Kids worry, "What am I going to be? How am I going to get through school? Am I going to drop out? Am I going to work my whole life in a fast food place? Where is the future?" Life is serious, but it doesn't mean it is always grim. They have fun, they kid around, they play ball, and so on.

JC: In your poetry, theme/message is paramount. Instead of *you* presenting a message, the voices within the poems paint a picture of life, a picture that can be interpreted in many different ways by those who read the poems. Given this, what overall messages do you hope readers ponder after reading the poems?

MG: I remember a kid once saying to me, and this was one of the best compliments I've ever gotten, "That poem, it's me. I felt the same way! I know that kid. I am that kid!" I said, "Thank you very much." That's what I'm trying to show, because when you're a teenager, you think, "Oh my, nobody knows how I feel; I am all alone." So, if there's one overriding message here, it's that everybody goes through parallel lives. Everybody goes through this. If you realize you aren't alone, there's help out there. There's a teacher or counselor who understands or a best friend who understands. Then you are not alone.

JC: Some of the poems in *Class Dismissed* are paired. That is, one persona speaks to or speaks about another (boy is stabbed, boy takes picture of him; girl has cross around her neck, boy steals the cross). Are these pairings a part of that belief in parallel lives, or did you have another reason for the pairings?

MG: People are connected. They are reaching out. They are trying to make contact. I remember one of my poems where a girl's mother warns her against kissing, and at the end of the poem that girl says that she'd take her chances, and Kevin kissed her. I started to think, "What would Kevin say?" And I thought he would say, "I wanted all these dreams, but I'm not going to get them. I threw up in biology. But, Lori loves me." They are beginning to reach out, to make friends. I thought, yeah, there is loneliness and it's tough being a kid, but they are becoming socially more adept and having a commitment to something more than themselves. I wanted this to come through in the poetry.

JC: When you use your own books with your own students, what sort of reactions do you get?

MG: It's funny. It's like at home you're no big deal. They say, "Oh, you write poems? That's nice." However, I teach one of my novels, *One Order to Go;* it is about a father-son relationship. After I introduce it and the students actually see the book, they say, "Oh my gosh, you wrote this book! That's cool!" That's the best compliment of all for me. I'm a teacher, not a star.

JC: One of the outstanding characteristics of your work is powerful use of simile, similes that mushroom into universal images. For example, in "Susan Tulchin" (from *Class Dismissed*), friends parade their reading abilities like new dresses. Tell us about the creative process that leads to these wonderful images.

MG: Flaubert had a comment that he could see pages and miles ahead and hear the fall of sentences. Even when I speak, a lot of it, even if it is sports terminology or whatever, is metaphorical. That's also the reason for my bad puns. I don't see things just one way. When I do these voices in the poems, I first hear the voices in my head. To give an example, there is a poem about Raymond in which he sees everything in school as grapefruit sections: first period class goes here—second period class goes there. He says life is not like that. Your brain does not come in grapefruit sections. I just heard all that one day. I think metaphorically. This is a facility with words that I have. It's what I do.

JC: The last line in each of your poems is typically a short, tight statement from the speaker that sums up his or her outlook and situation. Is there a special reason for this?

MG: That is quite conscious. In a Shakespearean sonnet there is a two-line couplet at the end that is the zinger, that summarizes it. I call it a "kicker," something that will make the reader go, "Oh!" That is very conscious. It may be a reversal back to the first sentence. It may be something the reader won't expect. In one poem the girl works at K-Mart, and her last line is, "Check it out." It's a play on words. I want to end the poem on a resonant note where the reader will go, "Ooooh!" I know that's not a very sophisticated reaction, but I want the reader to be pulled up short.

JC: In *Class Dismissed II: More High School Poems* (1986), there is a lot more in the way of word play, double meanings, and so on.

MG: It seems for a writer the first book has to be serious about life.

But for the second book, I said, "Okay, you already have something published. Lighten up!" I also started to feel more at ease in my writing. I realized that not everything had to be the definitive statement of the world. There could be times, and this shows up in *Mr. Candler* (1991), when all a kid wanted to do was try out for the baton squad. This was based upon a real person I knew, a student who sat outside my office one day. I said to her, "What are you doing here?" She replied, "Mr. Glenn, please don't bother me. I'm so nervous. I'll die if I don't make this team." I knew there was a poem right there. Not everything has to be deadly serious. In this collection I lightened up a bit as a writer. I started to write more about various sides of kids.

JC: This collection is a much "softer" volume. There are more subjects about choosing a college, searching for love, moving to a new home, getting a first car—subjects that weren't touched in previous volumes.

MG: If it's not a contradiction in terms, unconscious design is probably the best way to describe it. I think that grew out of my feeling more comfortable with the kids. I couldn't be a teacher for over twenty years unless I liked the kids. I do like them. For all the bad headlines one can read, I don't see kids that way. I really don't. I look at them almost as my own.

JC: Another characteristic of your work is that you are able to make larger issues, world or general social issues, very personal in the space of just a few short lines. In "Jay Stone" (from *Class Dismissed II*), for example, the speaker starts talking about world starvation and fighting in the Middle East, and a few lines later we are into the speaker's own life, a life in which these problems appear on a smaller scale.

MG: My thinking on this is that teenagers believe that the sun rises and sets with their permission. The world revolves around them. Everything is translated in terms of their own needs, panics, joys, and they see the world as there to serve them. Some of them are not very worldly; everything gets interpreted back to their own selves. One of my favorite poems is about the boy who talks to his grandfather about the numbers on the old man's arm. I remember hearing stories like that from my own father, and I remember reading articles in newspapers about that—about the Nazis putting these identification numbers on the arms of people in the concentration camps. This is probably the biggest evil in the twentieth century, but the kid in the poem translates it all in terms of himself. Teenagers relate everything personally and intensely. I think that is why I choose to structure the poems in this way.

JC: In your recent work you have also experimented quite a lot with the shape of poems and arrangement of words within them.

MG: I like words. I like crossword puzzles and other word games. When I was in college I remember going to the print shop where they had one of the old linotype machines. When I worked on the paper, I had to "physically" put the paper to bed on this linotype machine. This was before computers, and I'm sure this is why today I have such a rage at all these machines. I could really get my hands dirty with type. I think I just got the idea to experiment with the shape of words from these experiences. I think use of shape adds much to the meaning of a poem. In one poem when a girl track star says she comes through the line, through the tape a winner, and you can see the tape take form on the page, this is powerful. In my mind I pictured this scene painted with words. It just adds a whole new dimension to the lines. Also, sometimes I wonder if there is a sameness in the seriousness of the poems, especially in the first book. This use of shape is also an attempt to lighten things up, to make somebody chuckle: "Oh, isn't this cute; it's in the shape of . . ."

I just finished another book that is now in manuscript form and with my agent. In this book, I try a little more of this shape. I use a swimmer, a diver, and the words go down into the water like the diver goes into the water. It relieves a sameness in the poems, and that is conscious.

JC: The last section of *Class Dismissed II* shows a specific progression of time and focus: The reader moves through the senior trip, prom, graduation, and experiences a year out of school. This chronological sequence builds upon the blend of hope/despair that holds all together in your work. In the last poem of this sequence, the speaker, Miguel DeVega, has become successful in military duty, but he *still* laments that the recognition came a year after he graduated from high school. You just couldn't end all positive, could you!

MG: There are many times when the average kid, who is not a genius or a troublemaker, gets pushed aside. The schools are too large. Many of the schools here in New York have from two to three thousand kids. I have 150 students a day, five classes. A teacher can't be all things to all kids all the time. My classes are pen-palling with kids in a school in Nebraska. They sent us a letter and my students cracked up laughing because there are seventy-four students, total, in that whole school.

I think many students feel that they are alone and they are lost and they don't get the recognition they should. Again, if a kid can look at a poem and say what we mentioned earlier, "Hey, that poem is me. I'm not so bad," there's hope. Then maybe I have done something worthwhile. And this isn't all gloom and doom here. This is based on true-life experiences. I have students like this. People say to them, "There is no way in this world you are going to make it." Then I see them a couple of years later and they are in college or in the military, and they have succeeded. I'm impressed by what they can do, like the actions of the kid in that poem. It seems in high school unless you are really a standout or are in trouble all the time, you are not going to get noticed. I think this is another reason I write. I want to say to the average kid who is schlepping along, "There is an answer; there is hope for you." I don't see a lot of the poems as despairing. I see them as part of a growth process. The kids have to go through this.

JC: In *Back to Class* (1988), there is much more about the teachers and their thoughts. As a matter of fact, there are fifteen poems about teachers. These show the same range of emotions as do the poems from the point of view of the students.

MG: It is one of my favorite books because it shows teachers as human beings. They go to the bathroom; they have fears; they have hopes. I said, "I did this for students; what about the teachers?" In the first poem the teacher says he met a person in a health bar who said that he looked like an English teacher. And he wonders what an English teacher looks like. A noun for a nose? That is the focus of that book. The man is wishing that someone would say he looks like a big league ball-player. The teachers have the same needs. They need to say, "I'm doing something good. I'm helping. I'm a person. I'm not just somebody who writes homework on the board." This was a conscious attempt on my part to show that teachers are not gods. Like in all professions, there are great teachers, and there are teachers who have no business teaching, and a large measure in between. Students have trouble seeing teachers as people. I wanted to show that they have the same feelings about their lives that the kids do about theirs.

JC: In this poetry, free verse is an excellent choice for capturing the natural rhythm of voices and thoughts. This adds a special dimension, a special structure to the lines.

MG: The structure is implicit in the poems, but it is a different kind of structure. All my poems are between fifteen and twenty-five lines long.

Usually, my poems have a "kicker." Most often the poems will contain word play or a play on words to give another level of meaning. They are in the free-verse form. I know it sounds paradoxical, but there is a structure in the free verse according to how I hear it. I also like to pair an opening line with an ending line—for effect. Maybe a lot of this is because I don't know how to rhyme well! I spend a lot of time working for the right structure.

I just finished a six-year stint as a dean; as I said before, that position is sort of the academic version of "M*A*S*H*." We do emotional triage. Kids come in, and depending upon the seriousness of the problem, we take care of it. From this experience I wanted to do a book about a counselor and all the problems seen through the counselor's eyes. However, I didn't want to mention him until the last poem, where the reader gets to see him. This way, the reader would be able to understand his feelings not by what he says but through the kids' stories. That was my idea of structure there.

JC: Please tell us about your next projects.

MG: I just finished a book called *Where's the Class Of '78?* I wrote a group of poems about kids in 1978. Then I thought, "What will happen to them in fifteen years?" So, then I wrote poems about that. These are all paired poems. For example, there is a kid who used to like cars; he became an auto mechanic. It's like the end of the movie *American Graffiti* where we find out what happened to all the kids later on. I thought this would be a fun idea.

I have also finished a connected group of short stories called *Homeroom*. In the stories let's say the main character of one story has a last name that begins with the letter *A.* Then I go through the alphabet with character names in alpha order. There are twenty-six stories here in all. Also, a minor character of one story becomes the major character of the next story. All build upon each other.

I am most excited by my latest project. It's entitled *Can't Believe I'm Graduating.* I trace the lives of twenty-four students through their four years of high school. I hope this will be a successful book.

JC: Do you have a special message you would like to send along to your readers?

MG: Two things. One, thank you for enjoying the poems. Without the readership, I couldn't do the writing. And I'd like to thank my readers for sending along the nice comments they do. Two, remember that you are not alone. Your feelings deserve respect, and your questions deserve answers. What you are going through is important. Sometimes you may feel lost at sea and feel you are the only one going through something. But remember, you are not alone. Learn from your experiences and go on from there.

Select Bibliography

My Friend's Got This Problem, Mr. Candler: High School Poems by Mel Glenn (Clarion Books, 1991).

Back to Class: Poems by Mel Glenn (Clarion Books, 1988).

Class Dismissed II: More High School Poems (Clarion Books, 1986).

Class Dismissed: High School Poems by Mel Glenn (Clarion Books, 1982).

Aileen Fisher

Aileen Fisher spent her early childhood on a farm two miles outside the small town of Iron River, Michigan. She loved living her early life as "a child of nature," as she describes it. More often than not, her days were spent with her brother wandering the logging trails, playing with the farm animals, or swimming in the nearby river. These experiences have never left her. Her writings capture this freedom of childhood she so enjoyed and celebrate the beauty and magnificence of the natural world. In her writings, the reader will explore the domains of cats, rabbits, and a host of other creatures.

Aileen Fisher was awarded the National Council of Teachers of English Award for Excellence in Poetry for Children in 1978. She lives today on the outskirts of Boulder, Colorado.

JC: Aileen Fisher is a person of great curiosity about the world, and this curiosity is reflected in your poetry. *Out in the Dark and Daylight* (1980) is a collection that displays this curiosity and presents a related hallmark of your work: In this volume, no fewer than thirty-four of the 140 poems make use of questions to draw in the reader.

AF: The questions refer to the way I think. I suppose this is also because it's part of my belief that poetry should be full of wonder and magic for children. Probably some of the older poems, like these, speak to them just as much as the newer poems because of this. In my poetry I do what I think the kids will be interested in, which to me would involve a lot of questions and wondering about things. One of the difficulties these days is that because there is so much going on, children don't have much of a chance to be alone to think and observe. It's all a three-ring circus around them. In the poems they can ponder questions by themselves and have very private, personal readings. This is important. They don't get this from watching television; television is all one-sided. They don't participate with or through the television. It would be better if children would go outside for a walk or just run around. But I don't think children do that much these days. Children should spend their time outdoors looking at nature and wondering about things.

JC: At times you use a very structured pattern of rhyme in your poetry; at other times you vary the rhyme to give emphasis to the detail. This gives an air of unpredictability to your work.

AF: I think rhyme in poetry is terribly important. I get a good deal of mail from elementary teachers and the children in their classrooms. It is sad to say that not many of the teachers above the third grade say they use poetry in the classroom. The third graders are my great fans and are the ones I have the most rapport with. They love rhyme. And like me, they also love nature. Third graders are really great. I believe in using rhyme in writing verse; otherwise, you might as well shift to prose. It seems to me that poetry, especially for young children, demands rhyme because it is much easier for them to enjoy and remember the information in the poem—to learn the poem. When I grew up, way back when, we always had to learn poems. I can still say a number of them just because the rhyme pushes you ahead. The rhyme pushes children ahead and at times helps them anticipate what is coming up, and it's easier for them to read. I don't write much verse for children without rhyme. Also, rhyme is sort of a game. Children love games, and the fact that you can find things to rhyme that make sense is sort of a game. It has always struck me this way.

JC: One doesn't have to read much of your work before discovering that the magnificence of nature is the true focus of what you do. In your poems we find rabbits, snowbirds, stars, clover, wrens, frogs, and so on. Is this more a direct reflection of the environment in which you live, near Boulder, Colorado, or is it a reflection of what you consider the most appropriate subject for young readers?

AF: There are a number of answers to that. Nowadays, children are different from what they were fifty or sixty years ago because they are much more exposed to a wide range of activities, television, and so on. In school, the things they learn have made their ages different, in terms of what they know at a certain age. In other words, kids are growing up faster today. I used to write for eight- to twelve-year-old children. Now the eight to twelve seems down to six to eight. They just seem to know that much more. They are no longer, at a young age, walking in the wilderness, so to speak, but it's too bad they aren't, in my opinion.

If I get an idea, I start to write, and the structure takes care of itself;

and, the structure is usually provided by nature. Especially today, nature could well be the most important subject for children. The first book I wrote was *The Coffee-Pot Face* (1933). That was more about children's activities; it was not so much about nature. Now I'm older and I'm not around very young children all that often, but I know their interests and activities have changed. I don't write so much anymore about children and their families, but I do write about nature because it is something we all have in common. It is *the* universal subject. It is a subject all people can understand and enjoy. The way cities have grown, many children don't get a chance to be with nature all that much. Because a city is an artificial place, children grow up artificially. That is a great loss. Now they get nature second-hand through reading the poetry rather than going out and taking a walk. I believe children should not be sent to school so early. Let them get nature first. Let them figure out things for themselves. The wonder is there in everything if we just stop to take a look around.

As a child I was blessed. I was born in a small town, Iron River, in the Upper Peninsula of Michigan, and when I was five years old my father moved us to the country. My whole conscious childhood was country, and country has always been most important to me. I wouldn't live in the city for anything. I live now on the edge of town, but it's almost like living in the country. Actually, there are as many deer around as dogs.

JC: Tell us more about your childhood and how it influenced you as a poet.

AF: I simply loved the country. We lived two miles from town. I had a brother who was a year and a half older, and we did everything together. At that time there was still logging going on in the Upper Peninsula of Michigan, and we would follow the logging roads in the winter and go to where the wood would be stacked at the railroad and play there. Our whole world was nature. It was wonderful. We lived on the bank of a river and called our homesite High Bank. The river flowing below would freeze over in winter so we could skate. We would also swim in the summer, but water from area mines made the river red, so we had to go upstream. These are things that kids should be able to do today. We had chores to do, but most of life was very natural. All of this, of course, influenced me greatly as a writer and is in much of my work now, but the decision to be a writer didn't come until later. Also, when I was a young child my mother was a kindergarten teacher, and she had a flair for verse. So, I grew up with it. Mother could sit down and write a letter in verse. She was very, very good at it. She was a great influence on me.

I went to the University of Chicago after graduating from high school, and I started on a course of study which included Latin and Greek. I took two years of these classes and said to myself, "What am I going to do with Latin and Greek?" I had a friend at school who was from Missouri, and she suggested I go down to the School of Journalism at the University of Missouri at Columbia. She said it was one of the best schools in the country. So, after the two years I changed and went to Missouri. I always wanted to write, and I thought journalism would get me into writing. I graduated in journalism, but it wasn't the type of writing I wanted. I worked a while after graduation for a newspaper in Chicago, but it wasn't the kind of work I wanted at all. At that time I lived on the south side of Chicago but worked on a newspaper way up on the north side. I had to take the train to get to work each day. This gave me a lot of time to think, and I thought to myself, "This is no way to live!" I was so lonesome for the country that I would write on the train. Some of those verses I wrote on the way to work were published in *Child Life*, and everything mushroomed from there. I've never really talked about that much before, but that is how I got started as a writer. All my first verses were published in *Child Life*. By the time I had about forty or so poems published there, I decided to try them in a book. Those poems, along with others, became *The Coffee-Pot Face*. It was named a Junior Literary Guild Book, which also gave me a push. All those first poems were about simple things.

JC: Your poetry is full of joy, full of happiness, full of wonder. You do not deal with serious social concerns or the trials and tribulations of childhood.

AF: I don't think that is the purpose of poetry. What I wanted to do in poetry was give a lift, to put it quite simply, because life is full of wonderful things that pass us all the time. Especially in the country. I don't deal with serious things because in my childhood there weren't serious things, at least none we were aware of. Children become too serious too early today, and this is sad. My childhood ran along smoothly. The discipline was lax, but we were given things to live for and chores to do. My parents wanted us to enjoy life first. This, I think, is as it should be. I wish every child could have a natural childhood.

JC: Emphasis upon personification is also a major characteristic of your work as a poet. Practically everything comes alive and takes on human characteristics in the lines: Streets run, the sun goes walking, a lawn wears a jacket, and so on. This feature helps young readers readily identify with the material.

AF: I guess I just think that way. I think in terms of comparisons. I'd look at a field of dandelions and see them as buttons on a coat. That is easy for me. The comparisons should make descriptions that children understand.

I'm a very simple writer. I stick to the simple things. People are apt to get in trouble when they get complicated. I don't find writing difficult at all. All I need is an idea that would appeal to children, something they would have experience with. However, I do realize that all people are somewhat different. My brother is much more scientific-minded than I am. When we were kids, for instance, if we would see an anthill, we would sit there and watch all the turmoil of that anthill. My brother would get a bit of paint or something and put a dot on some of the ants so he could follow where they were going and see if they would come back. It would never occur to me to do that. I was more interested in the whole thing, not individual ants. I wanted to know how they could do anything without getting all mixed up. These are the different ways people look at things. I first try to remember my thoughts as a child, then consider the different ways people think and respond to the world. Then I write to that.

JC: Tell us more about what you do when you write. Any special habits or customs?

AF: Oh, yes. I'm very matter-of-fact in many ways. I like to be at my desk at eight in the morning. For years and years I've been at my desk from eight to twelve, either reading, writing, jotting down notes or verses—having a very good time. You see, I lived on a ranch for a number of years after graduation from college, and there was always a great deal of physical work to be done, such as chopping wood, trimming branches from the trees, keeping fires going, pumping water. Then, I had a much different life. I did those things after four hours at my desk. I had to write and read when I could find or make the time. Now, I try to keep my regular schedule. I really get great pleasure out of writing prose as well as verse. It's fun. I have had very good luck, too. I've been able to write for a living in one of the most difficult occupations. It is hard because it is so hard to sell what one writes.

JC: Which of your collections brought you the most joy?

AF: I guess I am most pleased with *Up the Windy Hill* (1953), but for a reason many will find to be odd. That was written in my early days, and it touched on a number of different things close to my heart. There are 130 to 140 pages of poems there, and the book sold when it was first issued for $1.50! To me, this is the thing. Give a lot for the money and not charge what so many books today cost, books with only twenty-some pages. I also illustrated that book with silhouettes, something we don't see much today. I couldn't draw illustrations, so I had to cut them out! I wish books for children were cheaper today. If they were, children and their parents would buy more and read more. Children don't have the opportunity to see a lot of books or receive a lot of books at today's prices.

JC: One of your more popular books of poetry is *My Cat Has Eyes of Sapphire Blue* (1973). This collection has twenty-four poems about cats and the various aspects of their lives. How did this volume come about? Why a whole collection about cats?

AF: I just love cats. As a child I had a very unusual relationship with them. My father was born on a farm in lower Michigan, and my mother was born in a city, Burlington, Iowa. In the city my mother didn't have animals around, but my father was surrounded by animals on the farm. These farm animals were animals for the outdoors; they were not animals for the house. His cat experience, for instance, was "all cats in the barn." They were cats doing jobs: catching mice and other unwanted creatures. It was the same way with dogs. We never had dogs in the house. They were also outside creatures. Animals, in other words, had to earn their salt. All of this led to my cat experience being different from most. Our cats were workers. They would have their little nests built in the hayloft of our wonderfully big barn. I would find these nests and pet the little cats and love them, but they were not allowed in the house. I would watch them grow up and would bring them fresh milk each day. I developed a real fondness for cats and loved putting together a book of poems about them. This was a way of capturing my childhood and also adding something my childhood lacked.

JC: In 1978 you were awarded the National Council of Teachers of English Award for Excellence in Poetry for Children. What was your reaction to this great honor?

AF: Early one morning I was sitting at my desk when the phone rang. Lee Bennett Hopkins was on the other end of the line, and he told me about the award and asked me to come to Kansas City for the ceremony. Actually, I wasn't terribly thrilled about the award at first, because if I had to go someplace and give a talk, for me that would take all the pleasure out of getting the award. I told him, half-jokingly, that I never travel. I told him, "What's more, I never wear anything but slacks and loud shirts"! He said that would be just fine. In the end, I didn't go to the ceremony. That's just not my forte. To go to a crowded airport is a nightmare for me. I don't enjoy flying. I just don't like to travel. What I like is writing for children and trying to make their world just a little brighter. Childhood is just a very special time.

JC: How would you like to see your own poetry used with young readers?

AF: Not much time is given to poetry in the schools today. First of all, teachers have to be interested. Teachers have to love it before that feeling can be transferred to the children. I think that when poetry is shared, the children should be taken outside where they can look at a variety of things and let their imaginations run. Something could be read in connection with those experiences.

Many children write to me and say that they want to be writers when they grow up. When they send me a note like this, I always send back to them an article I wrote called "So You Want to Be a Writer!" which was published in *Highlights for Children*. I send it so they can get a background and see that they have to practice writing, they have to read a lot, they have to enjoy writing. Some of these children will write poetry and learn to love poetry through that. I write back to all children who send me letters. That is important to me. Children are so special.

JC: Do you have a message you'd like to send along to your readers?

AF: It may sound strange to some children, but I would say each person needs to be alone a part of the time. Get away from the noise of the city and the television. Be by yourself outdoors for a time, in the country or in a park. The world around us is really a wonderful place, an amazing place. See the world and smell the world and wonder about the world. Experience the beauty in everything. And then if you can share your feelings with someone else, that will be an added delight.

Select Bibliography

Always Wondering: Some Favorite Poems of Aileen Fisher (HarperCollins, 1991).

The House of a Mouse (HarperCollins, 1988).

When It Comes to Bugs (HarperCollins, 1986).

Rabbits, Rabbits (HarperCollins, 1983).

Out in the Dark and Daylight (HarperCollins, 1980).

My Cat Has Eyes of Sapphire Blue (Thomas Y. Crowell, 1973).

In One Door and Out the Other (Thomas Y. Crowell, 1969).

Sing, Little Mouse (Thomas Y. Crowell, 1969).

Up the Windy Hill (Abelard, 1953).

The Coffee-Pot Face (McBride, 1933).

Karla Kuskin

Karla Kuskin has always been a person of great curiosity. As a child she longed to know just what made everything work, and this same curiosity is reflected today in the speakers of her poems. She writes for a younger audience, an audience of readers who will focus their curiosity and imagination on her skillfully crafted images.

Today, Kuskin views her writing as rewriting. She describes her own process of composing as splashing thoughts on a page and rewriting and rewriting until she is satisfied with the results. Her rewriting is the whittling away and paring down of words in order to present the message in the most precise, most economical manner possible. To her, writing is also the avoidance of clichés. Each piece should be a special spark of originality and have a refreshing flavor of newness so that young readers continue to find pleasure and surprise in words and language.

Karla Kuskin was awarded the National Council of Teachers of English Award for Excellence in Poetry for Children in 1979. She lives today in Brooklyn, New York.

JC: Your special vision as a poet can be seen in the typical speaker of one of your poems. It is an inquisitive vision, built by imagination but tempered by reality. Does this vision appear because you are a naturally inquisitive person, or is this combination something you have to work for in each poem?

KK: I suspect it is more natural in me than anything else. Starting in childhood, I wanted to know how everything worked. Really, how life worked. It is a part of my thinking process. We all express this curiosity in different ways. As human beings we spend a lot of time trying to figure out what in the world is going on around us. I try to capture this curiosity in my poems.

Photo: Nick Kuskin

JC: A hallmark of your early poetry was the creation of very detailed, very complete characters in the poems. Today, you seem less concerned with the characters themselves and more concerned with the thoughts and feelings of the characters.

KK: That's a good point. I would say that when I started writing and started doing books, I did what was the easiest for me, which was to write a bumpity-bumpity, very strong, very rhythmical, rhyming verse. There was a lot of that in my head; there always is. One of the simplest ways to write verse for children is almost cliché: You choose a funny name and write from there. Maybe it comes from limericks. I'm not sure, but it's been around forever: "There was a girl named Betsy Moo/ She didn't know just what to do." And you just keep going. That's boring. It's certainly boring after you have done it for the first twenty-five times. As I've gone along as a writer, I've gotten interested in ideas and more interested in playing with language and playing with rhythm and not making such regular rhyme schemes. What is more fun to read and listen to, to my ear at least, is the rather unexpected things that happen in the lines. That is not the case in my early, rather silly, very regular verse.

JC: In *Something Sleeping in the Hall* (1985), a wonderful collection of humorous poems, there are several poems that require the reader to complete them—either through responding to a question in the poem, or, as in the piece about the dog and the ball, the reader actually needing to complete an unfinished line. What are your beliefs related to getting the reader "involved" in your poetry?

KK: In the beginning, I don't think I really knew I was involving the reader. At least I didn't do it consciously. I didn't set out to say, "Oh, this is my part, and this is your part, and you will now finish the line." But, I noticed years ago that in one of my books called *James and the Rain* (1957), in the very last picture all the animals come in and sit by the fire, and they all supposedly go to sleep. However, there is one animal, a very small cat, that has one eye open. A very young child, about two or three years old, will spot that. An older child will take longer. An adolescent or older adult probably won't see it at all. I learned as I went along that I really was talking and telling stories to that young, observant eye and ear. It's a fresh eye that really sees and an ear that really listens to word sounds and the way language is put together. Some of me is always having a conversation with that consciousness, that very welcoming and alert consciousness in the very young child. Part of it, probably, is that I still feel some of that myself. I'm very observant of things around me and must have been as a child. I had parents who encouraged that, and I'm encouraging it now in other children.

JC: Any Me I Want to Be (1972) is a collection of thirty remarkable poems, each written from the point of view of the subject of each poem. Here, the reader can go inside the thoughts of a snake, a frog, or even the snow. In the introduction to this collection, you say you hope some of your readers try their hands at this same type of imagining and that you would be interested to see what they might produce. What did you hear from your readers?

KK: One of the reasons I wrote all of those poems was that I had done one similar verse before in the collection *The Rose on My Cake* (1964). It begins, "If I were a bird..." Children started using that original poem as a pattern for their own writings. So I thought, "Aha! There is an idea here." When we were little children, a lot of us pretended we were something else. It is also an idea that, if taken to the next plateau, is interesting and important. In order to be a feeling human being, you need to be able to understand that other people feel, too. Not everybody is like you, but everybody is worthy of serious attention. I have seen lots of classes use those poems and write after reading them. The children become jet planes and flowers and other kinds of people. Some are very original and some are sort of knockoffs of mine. I've had letters sent to me with poetry like this. However, I have seen more of these in the classrooms because I have visited so many schools now in so many places around the country.

JC: Related to this, how do you hope readers respond to your work?

KK: I hope they keep reading and writing. I loved reading so much as a child. Books have meant so much to me through my life. It seems such a gift to become involved in all sorts of literature and to be able to lose yourself in a book. Anything that I am writing is a little beckoning wave on that path: "Come on. There's a lot more down here. Keep involving yourself in it." This is what education is all about, and it is what poetry is all about. The more you read and the more you write, the better educated you will be and the better you will be able to communicate with people. You'll get more joy out of being human.

JC: In your poetry the reader is always linked somehow to the poem, in the same way the kite is connected by string to the person flying it in poem #13 in *Any Me I Want to Be*. Your poetry is an invitation; it is very warm, friendly. It invites the reader to jump right into the lines.

KK: I love, and have always loved, stories and poems that tapped me on the shoulder or whispered in my ear and said, "Come on. Let me tell you this. I have a wonderful story to tell you," and did it in the simplest possible way. I guess I take as much as I can from that idea when I write. I'm positioning myself to write the kind of thing I want to read, only on a level, of course, for very young children.

I think literature should embrace you and encourage you, particularly when you are young. Poetry should welcome you through its wonderful words and rhythmic language and wonderful sounds. It shouldn't be intimidating. It shouldn't, in any way, keep you out. If you're invited in, you'll continue and want to learn more and experience more. That is what I strive for in my writing.

JC: In *Near the Window Tree: Poems and Notes* (1975) you provide one of the most interesting types of invitation to the reader: You invite them inside your own thoughts as a poet. Here, you provide information related to how the poems were written, sources of your inspiration, and your own beliefs about the nature of poetry.

KK: I really think that when you write, in some way you are having a conversation with someone else, even though he or she is not there with you. Because one is always asked, "Where do you get your ideas?" I tried to answer that question. I really wanted to make the process of writing a poem seem as natural and accessible as possible, so I wrote those short introductions to try and show where each poem had begun in my head.

I have always been very aware of the sound of a writer's voice as I read. I suspect that is what encourages me, at times, to speak directly to a reader as if I were stepping out from behind some prose or a poem.

JC: In the introductory comments for the poem "The Rose on My Cake" (from *The Rose on My Cake*), you present your own formula for creating poetry, which includes rhythm, feelings, memory, rhyme, and imagination. Please expand upon these thoughts and describe your own process of composing.

KK: I always start writing poetry longhand with a pen, and I generally use a striped pad of paper. But, I jot down things on anything: on the back of an envelope, on scrap paper. I scribble verses or a rhyme or an image that goes through my head that I don't want to let go. I've got a zillion tiny pieces of paper all over the place that I'm afraid to throw out. They may come to nothing, but I have to keep them just the same.

The recipe itself really comes after the fact. I don't start out thinking that I'll start with two-thirds of a cup of word sounds and a quarter-stick of rhythm and put them together. I know that when I look back at what I'm doing, those are the elements that go into my poems and are emphasized by me in my poems.

Of all those elements, rhythm is the one that is most important to me. That is true for both my poetry and my prose. Rhythm in language is one of the things that makes a poem a poem, makes a good story work, makes a joke work. If you mess up the rhythm, the results will be poor. I always have rhythms in my head. It's as if I have a kind of metronome in me. Often I try to break the rhythms that are too regular and not very interesting. While I'm not particularly musical, I will always remember the lyrics but not the tune of a song. I feel that my sense of rhythm has always been good.

I love words and language. The more I've written over the years, the more I've realized that I am constantly trying to say something the right way or to get it as close as possible to what I think is the right way. Finding the word or words that fit is almost a game, a game I love. At times the words light up in my head. At other times, they don't. Sometimes I find a word or phrase that I fall so mightily in love with that I know it has got to go because it sticks out and makes everything else look bad. That's an old law in writing: When you fall too much in love with what you have written, you have to get rid of it.

JC: In your process of composing, how much revision is typical for you?

KK: I am much more of a rewriter than a writer. I have thought that for a long, long time. My poetry is not written the way I write prose. I rewrite prose a lot more. When I'm talking with children I certainly stress the fact that rewriting is an important part of writing. It's work, but it's wonderful work.

JC: You have said that all too often children are not able to enjoy reading and writing poetry because they are smothered by rules and subject matters they don't understand. How do you feel children should be introduced to poetry?

KK: Very young children are often smothered by the rules. Start with song lyrics and jingles from television commercials, jump-rope rhymes—any rhythmic language. Short stuff, easy stuff. That is with little children. When I work with them I never ask them to write a poem. I ask them to write a very simple description of a thing or something they feel something about. They then discover that if written in a poetic form on the page, some of the things that they are writing are really poems because the imagery is so fresh and the rhythm is good. I think the rules should come as children go along, when they are ready for them. The rules of poetry should not be what you bump into as you enter the realm of poetry.

JC: Related to these ideas, what would you list as the most important ideas presented in the filmstrip "Poetry Explained by Karla Kuskin" (1980)?

KK: In that piece I talk about the elements of my own poetry and what I do as a writer. It really is an outline of how people can use simple, short verse and rhythmic, sometimes rhymed language to spark interest in poetry. I also present the idea that when children are writing, they should be discouraged from rhyming. Their rhyming is generally imitative, so you want to work more with imagery and rhythm instead. Also, I believe a verse is a very good way of telling a small story. Children can use it that way. And poetry is a very direct line to feeling. In the young, poetry is a good way of getting them to record those feelings, to learn to communicate with others.

JC: You have received many awards and honors for your work. Of which honor are you most proud?

KK: When I received the NCTE Award for Excellence for my poetry, I was very pleased. I had designed the original one. In my acceptance speech I said that if anyone had any other awards they wanted designed, I'd be happy to do them just in case. In the long run, I know the most important thing to me is just sitting down and writing. That is my reward. I'm very grateful for being able to do what I do. I once gave a talk to a group of children and started out by saying, "If you are writing because you want to make a lot of money, because you can win a lot of prizes—don't bother! Write because you need to put something down on paper."

JC: What is next for you? What projects are you working on at present?

KK: Roar and More, my first book, was reissued in a revised edition this last year. I also have a new book of verses called *Soap Soup* (1992); it is an "I Can Read" book of verse. *Which Horse Is William?*, a book I did many years ago, is back out in a new edition (1992), and *Dogs and Dragons, Trees and Dreams* (1980) is out in paperback. At this moment there are quite a few other books getting ready to see light.

Select Bibliography

Soap Soup (HarperCollins, 1992).

Which Horse Is William? (Greenwillow, revised edition, 1992).

Roar and More (Harper & Row, revised edition, 1990).

The Dallas Titans Get Ready for Bed (HarperCollins, 1988).

Jerusalem Shining Still (Harper & Row, 1987).

Something Sleeping in the Hall (HarperCollins, 1985).

Just Like Everyone Else (HarperCollins, 1982).

The Philharmonic Gets Dressed (Harper & Row, 1982).

Dogs and Dragons, Trees and Dreams (Harper & Row, 1980).

Near the Window Tree: Poems and Notes (Harper & Row, 1975).

Any Me I Want to Be (Harper & Row, 1972).

In the Flaky Frosty Morning (Harper & Row, 1969).

The Rose on My Cake (Harper & Row, 1964).

ABCDEFGHIJKLMNOPQRSTUVWXYZ (Harper & Row, 1963).

Alexander Soames: His Poems (Harper & Row, 1962).

In the Middle of the Trees (Harper & Row, 1958).

James and the Rain (Harper & Row, 1957).

Jimmy Santiago Baca

Jimmy Santiago Baca views his poetry as a vehicle for spreading compassion and respect among peoples. Baca draws the inspiration for his writings from his study of the lives of his ancestors, especially the Mayan and Native American peoples, his family—a wife, two sons, and assorted animals—and friends in his neighborhood in Albuquerque, New Mexico.

Baca writes for a decidedly older audience, those readers who have the capacity for understanding how one is able to grow from terrible childhood experiences. His writings capture the development of the human spirit, which Baca describes as a communal spirit shared by all in our universe. These shared experiences, these universal feelings, join in his poetry to form a message: First and foremost, all should be proud of who they are in life; all people are important.

Baca also believes the fulcrum of all existence is change. Readers of his poetry will view the agents of this change on a personal level as his own life unfolds in the lines and on a universal level as he writes of others and their struggles for identity.

Photo: Lawrence Benton.
Courtesy of New Directions

JC: An underlying theme in your work is that we must first be proud of who we are in life. It is a universal message, one that touches the hearts of all. Parallel with this message, you give—especially in your early poems—a detailed picture of your early life and experiences. You share the pride you have developed through some of your rough experiences and direct others to seek pride in their own lives.

JSB: There has been a trend in American poetry that has filtered down to the schools that says if you write about yourself, you can be accused of being indulgent. I think the word "indulgent" is being used improperly in these situations. When you find one of the huge, gaudy signs of a fast-food restaurant in the middle of a tropical jungle, that's indulgent. I think that the poets not talking about who they are and what lives they are leading helps create the mystique that all poets are strange people who should jump off bridges. For young children, they should know we do have families, we do have jobs, we're not making millions of dollars, and that poetry, to us, gives us a feeling of being holy. It gives us a feeling of being blessed in the same way all life is. In the Navajo way it would be called the "Blessed Way." In my early life, even under some terrible circumstances, there was an extraordinary beauty there. I want young readers to see that beauty can be found in all places in life. The Navajo have a great way of expressing this: If you are in an area where there is a drought, then you should become the drought. Rather than opposing the drought and causing all sorts of misery for yourself, you become the drought—and this is what I did in my early life and poetry. This helped me celebrate that aspect of nature in my own life.

Here is the other extreme to that. While you are often not allowed to speak of yourself because you would be described as indulgent, at the same time the market can become glutted with the fantastical lives of writers like Norman Mailer and Stephen King and others. It seems to be okay as long as it fits into the critique of magazines that are looking for sensationalism. So, how can it not be okay to talk about the really serious material in the poetry, which would include information about our own lives? That's a very strange thing. In England, for instance, it's accepted that a writer should objectify his or her own work and not talk about the subjectivity of his or her own life. In indigenous cultures, like in Mexico and Latin America, people celebrate people's lives; they give hope to the people who cannot for some reason or other experience what others are experiencing. It seems that it is just in our country that these "indulgent" accusations come through. In Latin America it is not so. People there take a poem written by Arenez and they meet at a coffee shop and spend the entire day discussing it. I wish I could see more of that here.

JC: Your poetry also alternates between the depths of despair and the heights of freedom—from the cleansing smell of the rain to the death of a man in prison. This range requires a good amount of emotional juggling on the part of the reader.

JSB: What I wish to do is invoke, if not provoke, the feeling of compassion in my readers. Just simple compassion for another human being in whatever I am writing about. Our American society has built itself upon the premise that success comes from isolating yourself from others, that you can have a big house surrounded by big walls and have a wonderful life and never think of South Central Street in Los Angeles. If my poetry can bring readers to South Central in Los Angeles and show what is running underneath the skin and bones of a gang member or the old man on the corner in such a way that the reader is not threatened by it, I really do believe this will connect us communally to a vision for the future. If we don't do that, then we risk having the psychic earthquake occur that we are now having. You have the people in the suburbs buying guns like they have never bought them before. And the people in Los Angeles, for example, are falling further and further in despair. Some of these people live in areas worse in many ways than T. S. Eliot's "Wasteland." They live in a place that, ultimately, is a dead space. And that place comes to be the center of their lives. It is a horrible thing to have to wake up to that despair and have it deepen every day. I want my writings to bridge all of this and make people examine their own lives and the lives of others.

JC: A hallmark of your poetry is your particular brand of simile. Simile appears as a weapon used to attack the senses of the reader. In *What's Happening* (1982), for example, the reader encounters eyes "like rifle scopes" ("I Applied for the Board"); iron bars "still as cobras" ("Steel Doors of Prison"); seeds "like sword tips" ("Ah Rain!"); violence "like a gigantic snake" ("Overcrowding").

JSB: Language is the most powerful gift given to us. If you have a strain of madness in you, in a very sublime and benevolent way, as I think I do, I thoroughly and blindly believe that simile and metaphor can pierce steel. I really believe that. I believe that the energy that goes into a metaphor or simile coagulates from all the cosmic debris. I believe that when all of this is concentrated, it is more powerful than steel. It is an extraordinary power given to us by the gods. All of this comes from a belief I have. I can give a summary of this belief by telling a story. Let's say there is a wild dog that has been bothering us and we have to build bars and put it into a cage. That's one way of approaching the problem. Another approach is to believe that if you come up with a certain type of metaphor and you can convey that metaphor in such a way to the spirit of that dog, then the best communication possible occurs and the problems will cease to exist, will dissipate. Then, if the dog does what you want it to, why would you need the steel bars? It is an exchange of energy between souls. Simile and metaphor help us communicate in a mysterious and magical way.

JC: It is clear that much of your work is being addressed to those of Hispanic heritage, but the lines speak to a much wider audience. The lines carry universal messages to all.

JSB: Ultimately, the message is that all of us are looking for home. All of us are looking for a way to be normal. All of us are looking for a way to make the most of this life and its gifts. Some of us do that by buying expensive cars, others do it by buying condos, and still others do it by going to Las Vegas or other vacation spots. I try to find the center place where all people come together. I believe that people in Chile and China and Mexico and Afghanistan can understand each other because there are commonalities that run through all their veins, through the experiences of all human beings. When I write about a particular experience or event or feeling, I try to hone in on the root at which all people can say that they have felt the same way. This root of how we feel about things, the root of what we experience, never changes no matter who we are or where we live. The idea of love is never changed. The idea of despair is universal. The *causes* of these are different, but the root of these is the same in all people, in all parts of the world.

Language is the bridge between black and white, between red and brown, between yellow and brown. It is always the bridge between people so that when you actually write you are not Chicano, you are not black, you are not white—you are a bridge, a bridge of energy. You suspend who you are for a moment and participate in the energy that is universal. When you are done with the poem, you are who you are culturally because that is what you have gone through and that is how you have lived. But the product of that is universally human.

JC: In your later poems you have moved to more of a focus on relationships. An undercurrent in your work now seems to be that it isn't what one has in life that counts; what counts is who we are and the relationships we have in this life.

JSB: Everything is a relationship. Everything is relational. No matter how much you wish to succeed in life, no matter how much a wonderful person you wish to be, no matter how famous or rich you want to be, none of that can happen in the context of isolation. I hope my readers see that message in my poetry. Everything occurs within relationships. There can be destructive relationships and very positive relationships. In *Black Mesa Poems* (1989), what I tried to show was that although I can write about my own feelings and my own experiences, ultimately everything tunnels as a tributary back to all the people around me. All the people in my community have poetic lives. I go into that harvest of fifty or sixty years of a person's life and try to come up with just one single strand of wheat. Then I write about that and show how I am connected to that strand and how my children will be connected to it, and how the people before me were connected to it. This is the panoramic tableau of human experience. A poet has to write within a communal sense. If people depend too much on the glow of plaques and awards, all those things will take them farther and farther away from those people who mean something to their lives. My family is the blood of my life. I have a wife, two sons, three horses, and two dogs. I draw my strength from them.

JC: Fire is used as a recurring image and a symbolic reference in your work. Fire is everywhere, both consuming and cleansing.

JSB: The fire in all my work has innumerable connotations. You can take it mythologically back to the Toltecs, the Mayans, the Olmecs. All the way back to when it was prophesied that all the cosmos would be destroyed in the fifth sun, which would be fire. Mythologically, fire is regenerating the entire universe. Then again, you can take it down to the most minute metaphor of energy and molecules and how they are structured. In this sense, energy ultimately is some sort of divine fire. All the molecules are energy forms, and the universe and everything in it is fire: our breath, our skin, our bones, our hair, trees, grass. My work continually adheres to this image of fire because it has such a meaning of rebirth in it. We are constantly learning how to see again, how to feel again, how to change, and fire has that sense of change in it. Poetry is a constant search for harmony and balance in the universe, and fire brings it that much closer. Everything is evolution; everything is fire.

JC: How would you say you have evolved most as a poet? What changes through time do you see in your own work?

JSB: It is possible for everyone to become bored. I imagine those who load trucks with diamonds every day in South Africa get to a point where they look at a load of diamonds as no big deal. The essential pain and pleasure of life, the fulcrum of life, is change. When I wrote my early work, like *What's Happening*, it was for very specific reasons: to explore my early experiences in life, both the positive and negative. When I wrote *Black Mesa Poems*, it was to explore the surroundings and empathize with what others feel in life. In my poetry, I have moved from my inner soul to the communal soul we all share on this planet.

I also believe compassion should be shared by all daily, and I try to show this now in my writings. Compassion is also a very necessary thing in literature. American writers call it giving voice to the lines. Indigenous people in North America call compassion a way of seeing.

In Latin America and Mexico, people see it as a way of connecting and blending into another life form, and my beliefs are most closely parallel with this view. In this sense, *Black Mesa Poems* was my attempt to become one of the watermarks on the canyon wall, to join into a community that was here long before I was and will be long after I am gone. I hope I have become a communal member rather than a single voice.

JC: Your newest book, *Working in the Dark* (1992), is a connected collection of essays. In this volume, you say how you used the language, and in particular the writing of poetry, to become reborn. Please explain.

JSB: As it says in *Working in the Dark,* all I ever heard when I was seventeen, eighteen, nineteen was, "Your feelings don't matter. Your experiences don't matter. Your ideas don't matter. What matters is what grown-ups believe, and you'll never make it unless you abide by the rules of our system." *Working in the Dark* was an adolescent, primordial cry that said, "My feelings do matter! My dreams do mean something!" I wrote it in a very spontaneous way. I wrote about the things I wanted to talk about when I was eighteen but couldn't because the system told me they were the wrong things to talk about. The book reaffirms the experiences of teenage people. The topics I choose in that book are identity and the fact that it is okay to be who you are.

I also say it is okay for poets to feel tremendous terror when writing poetry, because that is what it is supposed to do. It is not supposed to come to you in teacups. It is supposed to come to you with a dragon's flame from the cave. Poetry puts me into my own passage, and I also try to explain that in the book. *Working in the Dark* is an organic odyssey that reaffirms the values of teenagers.

JC: In the book you also mention a film being made about your life and work as a poet. Tell us about that and other projects ahead for you.

JSB: I wrote and am acting in a film that should be released in late 1992 or early 1993. It is a three-and-a-half-hour epic film called *Bound by Honor.* The movie is based upon the events of my early life and my coming of age as a poet. I have also just finished a book of poetry called *Healing Earthquakes.* This collection is about the destruction and creation of an individual on his path through life. I also have a novel called *In the Way of the Sun.* In the future, I want to work on some documentaries about bilingual language.

JC: Do you have a special message you would like to send along to your readers?

JSB: Just really believe in yourself. And be prepared to sacrifice an awful lot for that belief. Have blind faith that ultimately in the end all things will eventually recognize and come to accept you for who you are. You *are* important.

Select Bibliography

Working in the Dark: Reflections of a Poet of the Barrio (Red Crane Books, 1992).

Black Mesa Poems (New Directions, 1989).

Martin & Meditations on the South Valley (New Directions, 1987).

Immigrants in Our Own Land & Selected Early Poems (New Directions, 1982).

What's Happening (Curbstone Press, 1982).

Mary Ann Hoberman

For Mary Ann Hoberman, writing begins with yellow pads and fountain pens full of real ink. On these pads she sketches memories of a vivid and happy childhood that began during the darkest days of the Depression. She blends these memories with the perceptions of today's youth to build in her poetry the timeless experiences of childhood: being fascinated by bugs, playing games, getting along with siblings, enjoying the nature of animals.

Hoberman strives for a delicate blend of the silly and the realistic in her verse. She hopes her readers gain enjoyment through the play and repetition of words and sounds; at the same time, she hopes they will learn something new about themselves and the world around them. In both The Raucous Auk: A Menagerie of Poems *(1973) and* Bugs *(1976), for example, readers learn amazing and unusual facts from the world of nature.*

Mary Ann Hoberman today lives in Greenwich, Connecticut.

JC: Tell us about your early life and your origins as a writer.

MAH: From the time I was a very little girl, I loved to draw and make up songs and little stories. I always knew, although I don't quite know how, that I wanted to be a writer. There was never a question about wanting to do anything else. Not a children's writer particularly, but a writer nonetheless.

My earliest memories go back to when my brother was born, just before I was three. I can say that by the time I was five, I knew that that was what I wanted to do. I used to go out into the garden behind our two-family house in New Haven, Connecticut, with an imaginary playmate whom I made my older brother. I had a real younger brother, but in my imagination I also had this older brother. I would go out in the

Photo: Gretchen Tatge

garden with him and tell him stories and play with him. And I would also tell my real brother stories. I remember my father was very proud of me for making up stories and songs, and he would have me sing the songs for his friends sometimes. He turned me into a real show-off. I can remember exactly the ages when all these things happened, because my family moved around a great deal. This was during the Depression, and we moved a lot because of my father's jobs. Today, my own children and my husband can't fix their early memories in the same way, because my husband grew up in one location and our children, after we moved to Greenwich, lived in the same house from a very young age. I've always felt that in a way this permanence was a deprivation as well as a benefit for them. Moving around so much as a child helped me to connect specific events and feelings with the age I was when they occurred, and these time-specific memories have helped me as a writer.

Anyway, that's my very early life. I was making up stories even before I could write. And then once I could write, I was always writing things on scraps of paper. This was during the Depression and it was a great luxury to have blank paper, so I would write mostly on the backs of pieces of mail that came. I remember being very thrilled when the bulletin from our Temple would come because it was printed on only one side of large sheets of heavy paper, so I had the entire other side all to myself. On birthdays or holidays when I was given a drawing pad with pure white paper, it was just the biggest treat in the world.

JC: What were your first pieces to be published?

MAH: I don't remember having any kind of school papers or publications in grammar school. The first publications of mine were probably in junior high school. In high school I worked on the school newspaper. I wrote light verse for the paper, and in my senior year, I wrote little two- and four-line verses to introduce the different sections of our yearbook. I also started writing what I considered more serious poetry in high school but didn't do very much with it. I kept most of it in private. I had sent out stories to the *New Yorker* before I started writing for children, and they came back as fast as I sent them out. I didn't publish any adult poetry until many years later, but I was writing all the time.

JC: How did *All My Shoes Come in Two's* (1957) grow from these early writing experiences?

MAH: That was my first book. My husband, Norman, illustrated it. As a matter of fact, he illustrated the first four out of five books that I wrote. Norm had just gotten out of the Air Force, and we already had our first child, who was born while we were stationed in Newfoundland. After his discharge, Norm decided to use the GI Bill to go back to school, so we came to Harvard, where he attended the architectural school, and we got a place to live nearby in Watertown. By then we had our second child. I can remember precisely the genesis of *Shoes*— and I always tell this to children when I go into the schools—it was autumn, when a lot of my good ideas come. I was pushing the two babies in a carriage along the street in Watertown and kicking up the leaves as I walked along, and this little couplet came into my head as I kicked up the leaves: "All my shoes come in two's. All my shoes come in two's." And I said to myself, "That would be a wonderful title for a children's book." I went home and thought about this. I already had an initial idea about what I wanted to do. In those days children wore high shoes above the ankle. I had observed that as soon as I would lace up my little girl's shoes and get them tied, she would struggle to get them off again. They were really her favorite toys. It occurred to me that shoes were very interesting to children. So I proceeded to write ten or so poems about different kinds of shoes, and my husband did the illustrations for them. We sent them off to Little, Brown, the Boston publisher, because I had been doing some freelance proofreading and editing for them to earn a little bit of money while Norman was in school. But I hadn't done any work in the children's department. I knew nothing about the children's department at Little, Brown or anywhere else, but I thought that it was as good a place as any to send them. Just at that time the late Helen Jones, my beloved editor, had decided to go in more heavily for books for younger children. So, our book got to her at just the right time.

After we sent it, we didn't hear anything for months, and I had almost forgotten all about it. By this time we had moved to Cambridge into a house about two blocks from Harvard Yard, where Norman was still in school. One day the mailman came and delivered a letter from Helen Jones accepting our book—the first place we had sent it to! By then we had a third child, but in my excitement I forgot completely that I had these little babies napping upstairs, and I went racing off to Harvard to show the letter to Norman, leaving all three kids alone in the house! It was one of the high moments of my whole life. However, in her acceptance letter Helen Jones also said that ten poems weren't enough for a whole book and asked me how long it would take to write about ten more. This was maybe on a Monday. I called her and said, "Would Friday be all right?" I suppose I was just in a dreamland at that time, but in those days I could write that easily. I wrote when the children were asleep. I was so used to using every spare minute of my time. Often I would get up in the middle of the night and go into a quiet room just so I could have five minutes alone to write. In this instance, I don't think I got ten poems done by Friday, but I did write them very quickly. In those days, when I was a very serious young woman, that kind of verse seemed to me something a person did right off the top of her head. *Real* writing was something that required deep, serious thought, but this type of writing I could just whip off. And I was making up poems for my own children all the time. A lot of the poems that were published in *Hello and Good-by* (1959) were composed in my head at this time.

JC: How would you say you have changed or evolved most as a poet from the time you were writing these first verses?

MAH: Well, for one thing, I don't usually turn out poems quite so rapidly any more! But changes through time probably have the most to do with a growth in self-confidence, and trust, and practicing the craft.

However, I've lost things too, I think. I have written lots and lots of poems for children, and most of them have come out of my own recollections of childhood. I think in the process that I've used up some of my memories. I'm also a lot farther away from my own childhood now, and this really makes a difference. At the same time, the self-confidence and the development of the craft of writing have both grown for me. Events of childhood may not be as fresh for me today, but my ability to develop my ideas and observations has become more powerful. I think many children's writers also feel the same way I do in that my childhood was very, very vivid to me. Perhaps nonsense was more available to me when I was first writing. I made up a lot of words and situations, which I don't seem to do as much anymore. Like most writers, at times I feel I'm dried up. At other times, ideas come in a rush. The older I get, the more thankful I am for whatever gifts I have. Writing for children has opened up so many worlds for me; I feel very, very lucky.

JC: You mentioned before about sneaking off to get a few minutes alone to write. How have your work habits as a poet changed?

MAH: Unless I'm working on a particular project, I don't sit down every single morning to write. I make up a lot of my poems when I'm walking or driving. A line will come to me, and that will be the grain of sand that starts the pearl in the oyster. I don't always have to be sitting at a desk to write. I can't write on my computer. I can't compose directly on it. I use it for typing up the finished material. For years I could only write with a fountain pen. I'm a little more flexible now, but I still prefer a fountain pen—with real ink. It's important for me to feel that ink flowing. Yellow legal pads and fountain pens call forth my creative juices. And I like to write in the sunshine. I'm one of those Leo people who crave the sun, and I gravitate toward the sunlight as it moves through our house.

JC: How do you hope readers respond to your work? For you, what would be a good reaction to your poems?

MAH: I love laughter. Laughter is important to me when I go into schools to share my writing. The easiest way to get to the children is with something funny, so I might start with a funny poem, but that isn't all that I want to do with them. I like children to respond and start talking to me. I go into schools a lot, and I enjoy most working with small groups. The children sit on the floor, and I sit on a little chair, and we build a real exchange of ideas. It's great when they start to chatter and tell me about a pet or a brother or sister after I've recited a poem about the same subject. That's the point of it—to get them to connect their experiences with my poems. I also like them to be surprised, and I enjoy hearing a little gasp when something they didn't expect appears. I also like their eagerness to learn poems and to participate in them. Many of my poems are participatory in nature, and I share these with the children for that reason. I look out at their faces, and I love it when I spot a child who is really responding in a creative way, when they tell me that he or she wants to do this too or that they, too, have written a poem. Maybe something I am doing for them there is reinforcing their desire or making them think, "Yes, this is a possibility. I too am going to write more." I hope my visits help it all come alive and provide some kind of connection to their own dreams and imaginations.

JC: In these situations you are influencing their writings and their attitudes about language. What and who would you say were the greatest influences upon you as a developing writer?

MAH: The biggest influence? Fairy tales, no doubt about it. I have always loved them. I had very few books of my own when I was little, it being the Depression and all. However, as soon as I could use the library on my own, I would come home with as many books as I could carry, and often they would be collections of fairy tales.

When I was a little older, I got a copy of Louis Untermeyer's anthology of modern American poetry and memorized much of it. I still have that copy, and I still know many of the poems in it by heart. I wasn't read to a great deal when I was a child, so I didn't know many young children's writers until I was an adult and reading to my own children. Edward Lear, Lewis Carroll, and A. A. Milne are my three touchstone children's poets, and these writers, along with Vachel Lindsay, Emily Dickinson, and Wordsworth, all have been important to me in my writing for children. That's quite a mixed bag, I know!

JC: Your poetry operates splendidly on many levels because one group of readers can be delighted by sounds, rhythms, and elements of rhyme found in such poems as "Combinations" (from *Bugs*) and "Fish" (from *Yellow Butter, Purple Jelly, Red Jam, Black Bread*, 1981), while other groups of readers will be lost in thought while reading poems like "Changing" and "Brother" (both from *Yellow Butter*). Just how do you achieve this universality in your work? Is it the "neutral" speaker (not of a particular sex or age group), or is it something else?

MAH: Although there are some obvious exceptions, most of my poems speak out of a sense of interest in and wonder at the world and its creatures that has nothing to do with a "gendered" observer. I think this is because even though I was aware of and undoubtedly absorbed many of the common sexual stereotypes as a child, at the same time I rejected them and never entirely identified with them. From a very early age I was conscious of leading a kind of double life, one as a little girl and another as a being completely unbounded by age or time or gender. And I still feel that way!

JC: In my opinion, a poem that best represents your work is "Waiters" (from *Yellow Butter*), a poem about a young child dining out with the father. Here we find a metrical pattern that doesn't skip a beat, wonderful rhyme, wordplay, a universal experience, and humor. If you would, please choose a poem you feel best represents your work and tell us why so.

MAH: I also like "Waiters." I like to think of words with double meanings and then just fool around with them. Sometimes I end up with a poem! Many of my poems are like puzzles, which isn't surprising, because I adore crossword puzzles and all kinds of word games. Many children do, too. It is so much fun to ask children to read these poems. Eventually one of them will say, "Oh!" when he or she gets what is going on. I love that.

I think *Hello and Good-by* is my favorite of all my books. I wanted it to be a small book, child-sized, and to contain all of the poems I wrote for my own children when they were very young. Helen Jones did me a great favor by publishing it, because in those days children's poetry just didn't sell very well. I also love Norman's illustrations in that book. One of my favorite poems is "Brother," which has been very much anthologized. It contains a lot of wordplay, it deals with a universal situation, it's funny, and it rhymes! It's the kind of poem I like to take into the schools for younger readers. None of the work I do in the schools ever comes consciously to me when I write the poems; it is only when I am actually there that I see how to share them with the children. There are always little tasks I set for myself and games I play with myself while writing my poems, and this is what I talk about with the children. With "Brother," they have it memorized after we say it once or twice. It is so regular in rhythm and rhyme, both excellent mnemonic devices.

I also like "Snow" from the same collection, and I like reciting it to children. I don't know if it would occur to anyone else to say it the way I do, but it is really a chant to be said very slowly and deliberately and with great emphasis upon the rhythm. I want children to hear the pulse of regular rhythm. Little children respond beautifully. They think, "What is this grown-up person doing talking in that funny kind of way?" Then they poke each other and giggle. But before you know it, they are chanting the words along with me. The last poem in that book, "It's Dark Out," is another of my favorites, and it too is a chant. That poem evokes to me all the winters of my childhood.

JC: Your poetry is both accurate and realistic when it comes to the facts included about a particular subject of a poem. In essence, readers can be thrilled by the combined elements of the poem and be taught interesting facts about the subject at hand. In *The Raucous Auk: A Menagerie of Poems,* for example, a reader discovers information related to everything from giraffes to whales. In *Bugs,* readers learn of the life cycle of the mayfly. Tell us how these poems come about. Do you start with a list of facts related to each subject, or the other way around?

MAH: For *The Raucous Auk* and *Bugs* I sat down and did what for me is real research before beginning the poems. For *Bugs* what I did was get one of those little plastic bug boxes and put a series of bugs in it so I could study them one by one. Some of these captives evoked poems. When I needed additional bugs, not just the local ones, I went to the library and set myself the task of writing a bug poem a day, using books and pictures. I'd look up whatever bug I wanted to write about and get some facts about it. Then, I'd sort of mull over the information until a poem came out of it. Some bugs caught my imagination; some bugs didn't. I learned all about cockroaches and locusts and once again celebrated the ant, an insect that I write about often. Children's science books are great for me, being a nonscientist, because I get a lot of information in a form that I can understand.

For *The Raucous Auk,* I went to the zoo. I'm a great fan of zoos, and wherever we go when we travel I have to visit the local zoo. My favorite one of all is the Bronx Zoo, which is only half an hour away from my home. For *Auk* I went there a number of times while I was writing it, and I would just sit in front of the animals until a poem came. I remember watching a huge brown bear walking around on two feet after being down on four feet. That bear impressed me, and it later appeared in a poem. I also wrote the poem about snakes after sitting in the snake house and watching a pair of them curled around each other.

JC: You use space and word/line arrangement in wonderful ways. In *A Little Book of Little Beasts* (1973), for example, the word arrangement of "Rabbit" forces the reader into a very staccato reading, a reading that mimics the nervous, jerky motions of a rabbit sneaking a bite to eat. In "Worm," the words are spread out to look like the segments of a worm's body. What is your philosophy related to space and line/ word arrangement in your verse?

MAH: I spend a lot of time thinking about those areas. I have always enjoyed shaped or patterned poetry. In specific instances, I'm very interested in the shape of a poem and how it relates to both its subject and to its language. I like variety. I like to experiment. I tend to use punctuation very sparingly, preferring to let the line divisions and the voice of the poem do the work. But at other times, for a regularly rhyming poem, I use the standard line pattern. Again, it's the poem itself that suggests how it should look on the page. That's another consideration, laying out the poem so that the reader can be helped by visual cues to hear how it should sound when read aloud. Also, it is boring to see a series of poems all laid out in the same way. For some poems, children will get more out of them if they are spaced in a visually striking way. For example, in "Rabbit" I was interested in having those "bits" act as a "spine" right down the middle of the poem to make a visual treat for the readers. That was how I wrote the poem; that was its purposeful arrangement. The repeated "bits" form the literal and figurative spine of the poem. When I go into the schools and present this poem, I have the children count the "bits" as I read it. It becomes a game, but at the same time a lot of mind work is going on. Learning our language can be fun for children.

JC: Your use of repetition in the poems is very pronounced, very pleasing to the ear. What do you see as the role of repetition in your poetry?

MAH: Whenever I talk to parent groups or teacher groups about sharing poetry and getting the children to join in, I always talk about the importance of repetition for young children. It is wonderful to have words come around again and have sounds that become familiar as the poem is read. I love refrains. I don't think familiarity breeds contempt; rather, it brings joy and pleasure. Repetition is a natural, logical part of language. There is always something very satisfying to me about an ending which comes back to its beginning so that a poem is rounded off in some way. However, I don't like repeating the same word when I'm rhyming. That's cheating in my book, even though Lear does it in his limericks all the time! Using repetition, if it works, is something that I am drawn to in my poetry.

JC: Many of your contemporaries go to great lengths to say that poetry for children doesn't have to rhyme. Yet, most of your work is a delicate balance of rhythm and rhyme. What are your beliefs in this area?

MAH: I agree with them. Certainly when I go in to do writing workshops with children, the first thing I say and stress is, "I don't want you to rhyme things. Let's forget about rhyme. Rhyme isn't poetry." I say this because children usually do it so poorly and it becomes an obstacle that gets in their way. However, as a child I was always rhyming things. I'm not sure how good it was or if it worked or not, but I do know that very few young children can handle rhyme well. It stymies them. I tell them if a rhyme comes to you, that's fine, but that is not what we are after at all. On the other hand, children love and adore rhymed and rhythmic poetry, as do I. Rhyme is one of the wonderful resources of the English language. And for better or worse, I am an inveterate rhymester! It is part of who I am.

JC: Fathers, Mothers, Sisters, Brothers: A Collection of Family Poems (1991) begins with a special poem ("What Is a Family") to set the stage for the rest of the volume. This is also a trademark of your work. Most volumes, like *Hello and Good-by, The Raucous Auk: A Menagerie of Poems, A Little Book of Little Beasts,* and *Bugs* all begin with one of these little poems. Are these like signatures for each collection?

MAH: It always seems to me that this sort of introductory poem serves to unify a book. I want to give each book some kind of unity. It's just a matter of form, a way of further defining and clarifying what the book is about.

JC: Fathers has subjects related to families (siblings to separations) and varied forms within the verses (the four-line "Sometimes" to the complicated "Dinnertime"). The collection also looks like an evolution for you. Most poems here are more detailed, much more intricate.

MAH: This collection is something particularly close to my heart. I've had the idea of doing a book about families for a good number of years. For this one I wrote twice as many poems as we finally included. I have always romanticized the family. We had lots of relatives when I was a little girl, and I loved it when they came to visit. Some were poor, some were rich, and some were very odd. I also enjoyed visiting them to see other kinds of lives that were connected to mine in some way. I loved the idea that the whole world is one family. Once I started to write these poems, the book quickly came together because I had so much material, most of it out of my own childhood. But, I also wanted to make sure that it touched on the way families are today. I didn't want any children to feel left out because they didn't have a father living at home, for example. That's why I wrote the introductory poem which asks what a family really is. I wanted every child who read the book to have the feeling that no matter what kind of a family he or she had, it was a valid and valuable one. I know there are things in this book that don't relate to all children. How could they, given the diversity of families today? But I wanted every reader to find something that spoke directly to him or her, and I hope I have succeeded.

JC: On several occasions you have mentioned that with young readers, poetry should not be studied until it dries up and blows away. How would you like to see poetry shared with young readers?

MAH: I would like to see poetry read every single day. Make it a daily routine or event. I'd connect it with all kinds of other things they are studying. For example, in my own work, *Bugs* could be used in science classes. Poems can be used everywhere. This is part of the whole-language philosophy, where you cross-fertilize ideas. Poetry is both subtle and simple; often it can get difficult concepts across very effectively.

I also wish children would write more, of course. Write everything! Not just poetry, but stories and plays and essays. Memorizing poetry is absolutely a joy, and children have such wonderful memories that they can do this quite easily. I would also have children make their own anthologies or scrapbooks of their favorite poems and books of their own poetry. It just seems to me it should be incorporated in all areas. Poetry is a very civilizing thing.

JC: What is next for you? What other projects are on the drawing board?

MAH: Right now I'm putting together an anthology of children's poetry. Also in the works is an anthology for older kids, high-school- or college-age. Also, because so many of my poems have gone out of print, I'd like to put together a big collection of them to restore them to life! It's sad to me that many of my early poems aren't easily available to today's readers. I'm very busy right now in many different areas. But my writing for children will always be a very important part of my life.

Select Bibliography

Fathers, Mothers, Sisters, Brothers: A Collection of Family Poems (Little, Brown, 1991).

A Fine Fat Pig and Other Animal Poems (HarperCollins, 1991).

Yellow Butter, Purple Jelly, Red Jam, Black Bread (Viking, 1981).

Bugs (Viking, 1976).

Nuts to You & Nuts to Me: An Alphabet Book of Poems (Alfred A. Knopf, 1974).

A Little Book of Little Beasts (Simon & Schuster, 1973).

The Raucous Auk: A Menagerie of Poems (Viking, 1973).

Not Enough Beds for the Babies (Little, Brown, 1965).

Hello and Good-by (Little, Brown, 1959).

All My Shoes Come in Two's (Little, Brown, 1957).

Myra Cohn Livingston

Myra Cohn Livingston is a poet's poet. It seems that whenever a statement is needed about a new book of poetry or a response to something controversial is called for, Livingston's is one of the first voices sought. She seeks to pave new roads in the world of poetry, which she has demonstrated by developing new poetic forms. Her poetry is characterized by devotion to form and structure, care and sensitivity. All elements blend to create poems that are vivid, unforgettable. In this poetry, she never speaks down to her readers; at the same time, the reading is not made easy. Livingston carries high expectations for her audience and hopes all will become actively involved in the lines.

Livingston also takes great pride in her work as a teacher of writing. She tells her students that laziness with the pen and quality writing do not marry, and this is one relationship that she will not tolerate—in herself or in her students. She has written and edited over seventy volumes of poetry, volumes that are a reflection of the child who lives within her. Through her guidance, many of her students have become published writers themselves.

In 1980 Myra Cohn Livingston was awarded the National Council of Teachers of English Award for Excellence in Poetry for Children. She lives today in Los Angeles, California.

Photo: Holiday House, Inc.

JC: I believe that all teachers who share poetry with the young should have a copy of *Poem-Making: Ways to Begin Writing Poetry* (1991). In it, you manage to explain, quite clearly, everything from elements of sound to figures of speech.

Poem-Making differs greatly from other books of the type in that you present how poetry *works* rather than just "how to do" certain poetic forms. However, there are those who say that younger children should simply write first and worry about this type of knowledge later. How do you respond to that view?

MCL: My feeling is that both are important. It is important not to start young children off with learning meter and form alone. In other words, what is urgent is to get them just to write. At the same time, many are capable as early as second grade of learning forms like couplets and tercets. *Poem-Making* is really for a little older child, nine and ten and above. Before that, if children are pushed into structured patterns, they are likely to use poor rhyme. If you tell children that they must have rhyme, they are apt to latch on to "fat" and "cat" and "mat." On the other hand, they love rhyme and can be encouraged to use it well. I think it is very wise to introduce them to some of these forms, like the couplet, very early. There have also been a few children I have worked with who really took to a necessity for learning meter.

There is also another factor that should be considered here: If a child has been read to well at home, the child will write much more easily. Children who have had good books read to them know instinctively what is bad, and the material won't please the ear. Then they get really frustrated and want to know what is wrong with the piece. So, if they can be taught some of the metrical patterns and the forms, they are much happier as readers and writers. I think, in essence, *both* should be taught.

At the same time, there are too many teachers who want the magic pills, who find it easier to give children an opening line, or fill-ins, or accept prose arranged as poetry. Then, of course, there is a whole school of poetry that says rhyme is dead and meter is dead—that both are something left over from the past. As far as I'm concerned, poetry is still a matter of music; the music must be in the poem. It can be made through rhythm, through meter, through assonance, consonance, alliteration. It has to be present in some way to make a poem memorable. Unfortunately, today if something has an anapestic beat and rhymes, some call it poetry. It is not. It's often simply verse. Too many people confuse the two.

JC: For teachers and younger readers who haven't yet read *Poem-Making,* please state what you consider the most important idea presented there.

MCL: No one, to my knowledge, has ever pointed out the potential and possibility of different voices, and that is the most important idea presented in the whole book: the idea that one can change a poem and make it much more meaningful through choice of voice. If a child understands the different kinds of voices that can be used, the knowledge will much enrich the child's writing.

JC: This is a very difficult concept for the young, and I think the way you explain it in the book is quite good. It is made quite clear.

MCL: A teacher can explain this by using examples of those voices children use at a young age. The mask, for example, or the voice of apostrophe. Young children use those voices continually. They pretend they are something or somebody else; they talk to something directly. These voices, however, are often lost at about eight or nine years old.

JC: An outstanding feature of your work as a poet is that you use so many different speakers yourself. What is it about you that enables you to create these different speakers when others cannot? In other words, how do you "write so young"?

MCL: I think there is a child within me that responds. I also think back to my own responses to things when I was a young child. Naturally, I cannot do this as well as I did when I was eighteen, but when I look at a subject I wonder how a child would respond to it. When I was very young I wrote *Whispers and Other Poems* (1958). I was very near to childhood then. Now I am not that close, yet there is a child living within me. I advise my adult students when I teach at UCLA, "If there is no child left in you, forget about writing for children, because it will be difficult to achieve."

JC: In terms of form and structure, I would say that the most remarkable characteristic of your work is that your poetry is not predictable. Each poem is fresh, unique, styled to the demands of the subject matter. This is especially true in terms of sound effects: rhyme, rhythm, alliteration, assonance, onomatopoeia. It is also true in terms of shape/arrangement of the poems. Do you suppose this is because, as you say in *Poem-Making,* that for you finding the appropriate form for a poem is one of the most difficult tasks you face as a writer and you spend so much extra time searching for just the right form?

MCL: Absolutely. I think the poet's art is to make the subject of the poem and the form in which it is put mesh perfectly. One can try a poem in many different forms until it "comes right." Often, after I have finished a poem, I'll look at it and I'll say to myself, "This is awful writing. This is junk. You've fallen into verse again." I've fallen into verse because I haven't found the right form for what I wanted to say. That's why I think it is important to learn form.

JC: Why does it seem that so few writers, both students and professionals, take this extra time to search for this perfect blend of subject and form?

MCL: Because many simply do not know anything about the craft. That is the problem. Many think that all there is to writing a poem is to spill out one's guts on the page and maybe rhyme once in a while or avoid rhyme altogether because it is considered passé.

JC: Your comment about your own struggle for form seems odd from a writer who has mastered everything from riddle poems to pure lyrics. Could you illustrate this comment by telling about a time when you "struggled" in your search for just the right form for a particular poem?

MCL: I can give a very good example of that. It happened when I wrote *Space Songs* (1988). Before *Space Songs,* when I wrote *Earth Songs* (1986), I invented a form because I needed strong sounds to go with the earth. In *Earth Songs* you may have noticed that in all the stanzas the last word of the first line rhymes with the first word of the second line; the last word of the second line rhymes with the first word of the third line. The same pattern continues for the third and fourth. At the end of the fourth line, the last word here rhymes with both the first and last word of line five. It gives a very rich sound. I thought this form would also be wonderful for *Space Songs,* but several big problems presented themselves. For example, words like Sea of Tranquility, Jupiter, Pluto, Saturn, meteorites, quasars, neutron stars, comets, asteroids, and so forth all have varying rhythms. How was I going to put all those into the right form?

The first poem I wrote for *Space Songs,* "Stars," wasn't published in the book. It was published in *Cricket* magazine. I was absolutely amazed when Carl Sagan wrote that if you pick up a handful of sand there will be about ten thousand grains in it, and there are more stars in the universe than grains of sand on earth. It just boggled my mind. But after I wrote "Stars," I realized that it was written in quatrains. I couldn't write the other stanzas in quatrain, so I had to find a form that could embody these particular words. I decided to use a very loose rhyme form. It was probably one of the most difficult books I have written for that reason. Take the poem "Asteroids," for example. In "Asteroids" I had to talk about Eros, Icarus, Vesta, and Flora. Those are trochaic and dactylic words, and I had to have a framework in which to put them. It was a challenge.

JC: A great amount of time went into the arrangement of words in *Space Songs.* The shape of the poem is so illustrative of the material in such poems as "Stars and Constellations" and "Meteorites." That purposeful arrangement is another characteristic of your work.

MCL: Sometimes it just happens, but not all the time. Every once in a while a poem will come along, and I'll know that it needs a certain shape. This started for me when I wrote a poem called "Buildings" that appeared in *Whispers.* I wrote this book when I was eighteen. What I did in "Buildings" was my first use of this type of arrangement. It just came to me that the shapes of different buildings were needed. Perhaps it is more something subconscious that wells up in me.

JC: Another very special aspect of your poetry is that you don't talk down or write down to your readers. What are your views related to this?

MCL: I think it is a matter of respect for children. One must have respect for children and their feelings. If one does, then one will never write down to the reader. Writers should look at children and remember that they are very fresh in their observations. They haven't been clamped down into clichés yet.

JC: At the same time, some critics have complained that your work deals too much with the common, everyday events of childhood. What do you say in response to those comments?

MCL: Ninety percent of what our lives touch is the ordinary and the commonplace, and children are still learning about this aspect of life. Fantasy and nonsense are both rooted in the commonplace; it is a measure of our lives. I think the problem here is that if you are determined to make children giggle and get the quick laugh, then you are going to invent a kind of nonsense that will elicit guffaws. Many people in the television mentality want only the quick laugh. They don't want the thoughtfulness that goes into just observing a tree or an everyday experience.

JC: My Head Is Red: And Other Riddle Rhymes (1990) is a collection of twenty-seven riddle poems that are very entertaining. They also promote active reading for young readers. A good number of contemporary poets are writing poetry that requires this sort of interaction between reader and print.

MCL: I like the riddle poems because they require a great amount of thought on the part of the reader. The reader *must* become involved with the lines. But I am not in favor of something like giving a child a first line and saying, "You finish it." I don't think that is creative. More important time could be spent taking a child on a walk, an observation walk, and saying, "What do you see?" It takes a lot of work to teach reading and writing. You really don't teach writing; you develop sensitivity in the person. You teach the person to use his or her sensibilities, and then you teach forms in which to put those responses.

JC: In *Worlds I Know: And Other Poems* (1985), you use descriptions of such interesting characters as Nanny, Aunt Evelyn, Mary Lorenz, Old Sam, Grandfather, and Lena to create a world that all children know and understand. I know you dislike "preachiness" in poetry, but an undercurrent here and in your other collections seems to be that we can learn something from all people, like those you create here, and we should be respectful of others. Your comments?

MCL: I would never wish to be didactic. I don't think I did that consciously. These are all real people of my childhood. *Worlds I Know* is really *Whispers* rewritten. *Whispers* was written when I was eighteen; *Worlds I Know* was written in my fifties. I went back and kept thinking of [teacher and friend] Horace Gregory's remark that there were no devils in my world. I looked back at my childhood and realized that there *were* devils in that childhood. There were individuals I didn't like or care for, for many reasons, and others I loved. The people in this book are symbolic of the people in every child's life.

JC: How would you say you have changed or evolved most as a poet over time?

MCL: The child I was growing up in Omaha is not the child of today who lives in Los Angeles or New York or anywhere else. The world is not the same and children are not as naive as they used to be. They couldn't be, living with television, either in factual matters or emotional responses. They grow up in a different way, learning things that I never knew as a child. I was terribly naive, and yet there are some universals about life that never, never change. At the same time, it is very sad if we remain the same. Horace Gregory said there weren't any devils in my world because what I wrote was about the beautiful and the good. As I grew I discovered there are divorced households and many problems facing children today. So, why not write about these matters for children who are reacting to their environment and/or suffering and don't know how to express themselves? *There Was a Place* (1988) is directly based on this whole interaction with children who would say to me, "Well, for whom should I write a valentine? My father, or the man my mother lives with?" I felt there should be some voice for these children. Many people think of me as a poet of feelings and emotions. I guess I respond to the hurt, fears, and emotions of the young more than anything else. They are very real. Very, very real. And, there is no better way to do this than through literature. I hope my poems reflect this. I also think this makes some people uncomfortable.

JC: Please tell us about your work as an anthologist. How did this aspect of your work come about?

MCL: That happened because I was speaking at the University of California, Berkeley, about twenty-five years ago. One night Mae Durham, an editor and friend, asked me if I would bring some poems to read to a group of people. These were not my poems; we were just reading and discussing poetry of all types. When I finished my selections she said, "You should do an anthology." I said that I wasn't an anthologist and doubted if I could do it. She said, "Yes, you can—the way you select poetry, you have the talent." So I did *A Tune Beyond Us: A Collection of Poetry* (1968), and I have edited thirty-two more since.

I compiled that anthology with certain things in mind: Number one, I was annoyed with anthologies that didn't pay any attention to the great wealth of culture from all over the world that is in the United States. That is something that people are just starting to pay attention to now. I was very concerned about that at the time, so of course that book had the original Russian, Chinese, Japanese, and French in it. It was very well received—an ALA Notable Book. So a thought came to me: Why not put together some other kinds of poems? Of course, as I mentioned, I did many anthologies after that.

Number two: I think anthologies are a wonderful way to introduce poetry to young people, because if different poets are represented, a child can read through and say, "I love Valerie Worth. I'll see what else Valerie Worth has done." With the Holiday House series, I saw an opportunity to publish new work, so I wrote to all my poet friends and asked them if they would do poems for me or had poems already on a particular subject. Now, all sorts of poets send me material and ask me to consider it if I do a certain type of anthology. I read all these and have discovered that a lot of bad stuff is being written right now because these people do not know form. They have no background in poetic craft at all.

JC: Lee Bennett Hopkins says that he has what he calls his "take-out" poets. If he needs a particular type of poem for an anthology, he writes to them and asks if they can write that particular type for the project. Would you say the two of you are alike in this respect?

MCL: Lee is a very good friend of mine; I'm very fond of Lee, but I think we work differently in some ways. If I want something I send letters to twenty different people and ask if they have something for me. And, I teach. Sometimes I will use the work of my UCLA students. If one of my students has written an especially good poem, and if it fits in, I'll give the student a chance to publish it. That first publication is very important because until students have something published, they really don't know if they have talent or something worthwhile to say. Some of my students are in their seventies, and publishing a piece of writing is something thay have always wanted to do. Others are much younger and need a boost.

JC: What is next on the horizon for you?

MCL: I have a ballad about Martin Luther King coming out. I also have several anthologies in the works. I have about twelve books coming out in the near future. I can't bear to be idle.

Select Bibliography

My Head Is Red: And Other Riddle Rhymes (Holiday House, 1990).

Dilly Dilly Piccalilli: Poems for the Very Young (MacMillan, 1989).

Remembering and Other Poems (Macmillan, 1989).

Up in the Air (Holiday House, 1989).

Space Songs (Holiday House, 1988).

There Was a Place, and Other Poems (Macmillan, 1988).

Earth Songs (Holiday House, 1986).

Higgledy-Piggledy: Verses and Pictures (Macmillan, 1986).

Celebrations (Holiday House, 1985).

Worlds I Know: and Other Poems (Atheneum, 1985).

Monkey Puzzle, and Other Poems (Atheneum, 1984).

No Way of Knowing: Dallas Poems (Atheneum, 1980).

O Sliver of Liver and Other Poems (Atheneum, 1979).

4-Way Stop, and Other Poems (Atheneum, 1976).

The Way Things Are, and Other Poems (Atheneum, 1974).

The Malibu, and Other Poems (Atheneum, 1972).

Old Mrs. Twindlytart, and Other Rhymes (Harcourt, 1967).

The Moon and a Star, and Other Poems (Harcourt, 1965).

Whispers and Other Poems (Harcourt, 1958).

Anthologies Edited

Lots of Limericks (Macmillan, 1991).

Poems for Brothers, Poems for Sisters (Holiday House, 1991).

Dog Poems (Holiday House, 1990).

Poems for Grandmothers (Holiday House, 1990).

Halloween Poems (Holiday House, 1989).

Poems for Fathers (Holiday House, 1989).

Cat Poems (Holiday House, 1987).

Easter Poems (Holiday House, 1985).

Thanksgiving Poems (Holiday House, 1985).

Why Am I Grown So Cold?: Poems of the Unknowable (Atheneum, 1982).

Callooh! Callay! Holiday Poems for Young Readers (Atheneum, 1978).

Listen, Children, Listen: An Anthology of Poems for the Very Young (Harcourt, 1972).

A Tune Beyond Us: A Collection of Poetry (Harcourt, 1968).

Books about Poetry

Poem-Making: Ways to Begin Writing Poetry (HarperCollins, 1991).

Climb into the Bell Tower: Essays on Poetry (HarperCollins, 1990).

The Child as Poet: Myth or Reality? (Horn Book, 1984).

Valerie Worth

Valerie Worth was the ninth recipient of the National Council of Teachers of English Award for Excellence in Poetry for Children (1991). A true master of the lyric form, Worth's "small poems" have given to young readers great treasures: Small Poems (1972), More Small Poems (1976), Still More Small Poems (1978), Small Poems Again (1986).

A casual reading of these works might lead one to say that her poems are models of simplicity. On the one hand, they are simple in that they are not cluttered with lengthy descriptions or visually complicated structures. But through this simplicity, the poems are a masterful blend of poetic elements, all combined to produce poems that are anything but simple in terms of effect on the reader. The poems explode; they mushroom into sights and sounds. Readers of her poetry are awed by sensual imagery and breathtaking sound effects.

Today, Valerie Worth lives with her husband in Clinton, New York.

JC: You were chosen as the ninth recipient of the NCTE Award for Excellence in Poetry for Children. What was your initial reaction to that news?

VW: Great excitement and happiness. To be recognized by NCTE is a great honor. Also, I have had correspondence with two other poets who were granted this award, Myra Cohn Livingston and Lilian Moore, and it is really nice to be considered in their company. It was just a wonderful feeling. I do volunteer work every two weeks at a local thrift shop, and I was right in the middle of my work there when I got the news. That was very nice because I could share it with all of my friends there, and they were very excited too.

Photo: Temple Studio

JC: The writing career that has grown to this honor—how did it begin?

VW: I read a lot as a child. I read poetry, fiction, fairy tales—all kinds of literature. Many of the feelings I have for poetry came out of those reading experiences. I loved poetry before I even thought of writing it myself. My parents were also fond of poetry, and my father wrote poetry a little bit, too. He wasn't a published poet, but he wrote poetry all his life. I know that influenced me.

I think it was a feeling for words and images and all the imaginative material that was contained in the poetry I read that first gave me a feeling for it. I also think that my childhood was probably the most perceptive time of my life. Everything seemed so vivid to me then. In a way it does now, but it's not with the same freshness. I have always remembered the way I felt about things as a child. The world seemed full of wonderful things to look at and to think about, and I responded to that. I would recognize these things in poetry, but I also had a feeling that there might be something I could do with them myself along those lines. I did try little poems, just childish poems, at first, but as I got a little older I was more serious about trying to put into poetry some of the things I had felt about other people's poetry and some of the things I'd seen around me. I think it wasn't until I was in high school that I really discovered that I could write poetry in a way that measured up to what I wanted to do.

JC: Which poets did you read during that early development?

VW: I read children's poets, but I also read some adult poets like Carl Sandburg and T. S. Eliot a little later on. However, the poet who most influenced me was Rupert Brooke, and the poem of his that meant the most to me was "The Great Lover." That poem had a whole collection of wonderful images describing very simple things. As I read it there was just a special kind of recognition there. In a way, it has been the source of my imagery today.

JC: Please share more about your childhood and development as a writer.

VW: I was small for my age and was shy. I did a lot of things by myself. I wasn't really antisocial, but I very much enjoyed being on my own and sort of wandering around and looking at things or reading on my own. In fact, there were times when my mother had to push me out the door to play with other children. I had an enjoyment of solitude that encouraged my observation of all around me. These reflections were perhaps what contributed to my wanting to write and express myself in poetry rather than just through talking to other people. When you write you are by yourself, and you are sort of writing for yourself. When you're talking, then somebody else is involved, and that's a different experience entirely.

I really wrote nothing of significance until high school. Then there were a few poetry contests I entered, and I won awards in all of them. I was also one of the winners in a statewide poetry contest when we lived in Florida, and my poem was published in an anthology. Later, when I was in college, I had a story published in *New World Writing,* and that was my first really important publication. I also had a few poems published in *Harper's* in the 1960s, but I really didn't write poetry for children until later. Then, I tried sending my children's poems around for four or five years and had no luck at all getting them published. This is a good lesson for younger writers: Never give up!

When we moved to Clinton, New York, I met and was in a writing group with author and illustrator Natalie Babbit. One day I took some of my poems to share in this group. Natalie read them and then sent some of them to her editor, Michael di Capua. He liked them, and that is how *Small Poems* came about. That was the real beginning of my children's poetry.

JC: Today, one of the hallmarks of your poetry is splendid use of personification. In the verse, young readers discover furniture, flowers, and animals that all come alive. They jump from the page and give energy to the lines.

VW: I often feel a powerful personality in things that are either not human or not alive but have a kind of personality that could be equal to something human. Many objects have powerful presences and striking characteristics. Not everything strikes me this way, but in some cases certain aspects of these objects or animals catch my eye. Poetry is a very good way to bring out traits like this because it works with both reality and imagination simultaneously. The poet can combine the two and have something be itself and also be something else at the same time.

JC: Something noticeably absent from your poetry is people. While inanimate objects and animals come alive and seem very human, the only people present are the readers of the poems.

VW: For me, poetry deals with the world of the individual senses: things you see, hear, touch, smell, taste. When more people are involved, relationships are created that are dramatic and complex. It seems to me that fiction does better than poetry in dealing with those concerns because you have the scope to explore personality and deal with one person reacting to another or reacting within a group. I have written three books of fiction, and that's where I've worked on exploring the ways that people think and act. When I'm working with my poetry, it seems to be an intense focus and maybe a narrower one. I think for me to try to put people into the poems would somehow be too much. They would get too complicated, or they would get into patterns that I'm not really interested in dealing with. In my poetry, the only person is the reader, and I think that is something very positive. If only the reader is there, then that reader experiences everything directly and clearly, and there's nobody else around to get in the way.

JC: Of all the characteristics of your work, use of simile may be the most remarkable. These comparisons create images that remain long after the pages have been turned. Readers encounter such images as a safety pin like a thin shrimp, a cat's steps put down like playing cards, and a tractor that is like a grasshopper.

VW: Through simile and metaphor, the poet is able to express the nature of a subject by seeing it in relationship to something else. To show that one object might resemble something else could reveal unexpected qualities in both of them so that the reader experiences a revelation on both sides. Also, there is a lot of pleasure in discovering that two unlikely objects are in some way the same. A reader might never have thought of the comparison before, so when a poet points it out, suddenly it enhances both.

JC: In which ways do you hope readers respond to your work?

VW: I write about common, everyday objects and events. When you are working with objects that are quite ordinary and you make them seem unusual, either through comparison or personification, the effect can be quite startling to the reader. Maybe the reader will be surprised into seeing things in a new way. That reaction is very valuable, because if readers can begin to look at the world in a fresh way and to see things that are surprising and unusual, then that is a kind of new vision that the poem has given them. That, ideally, is what I'd like my poems to do. Even in a simple, everyday object, you can have surprising qualities you might never have thought were there—and suddenly they are there. I would hope my poetry would do that for others.

JC: Which audience do you consider the most important for Valerie Worth? Which readers are you most trying to touch?

VW: I write for children, but I also write for myself as I remember my own childhood. The experiences of childhood carry through to everybody, at any age, and I should think all people would find pleasure in either remembering or reliving these experiences. Also, I write a lot about the natural world, which everybody has access to. Most people like nature, and they respond to animals, plants, and scenery. If I wrote about a narrower range of experience, then that would limit the audience. However, writing about things that all have seen is a great way to reach people. And, these are the subjects I respond to myself.

JC: In this poetry, your use of rhyme is very subtle, very mild when compared to many contemporary poets writing for children and young adults.

VW: It is very hard to use a formal rhyme scheme. I think it is probably the greatest challenge of all in writing poetry. I find that rhyme gets in my way, because in order to fulfill the rules, you have to shape your words in a way that is not always how you want them to be. To my mind, rhyme is not really that necessary. What I feel is important is the sound of words. I can use these sounds with much more freedom, and I don't have to have them coming in a particular order or in a particular place. I use rhyme when it naturally grows out of the words I'm using. Sometimes it is a matter of chance that the words I want to use do rhyme or they do have similar sounds, and this is wonderful because the poem helps to write itself. Some poems really call for rhyme, and some are better without it.

This is also true of rhythm. Some poems take on their own rhythm, and in some places rhythm helps to emphasize the subject being explored. For instance, when I was writing about a clock in one of my poems, the poem ended up with the rhythm of a clock. As I worked on that poem, it took on that orderly rhythm not because I wanted to have order but because it grew naturally out of the subject. If the set form of rhyme or rhythm leads me to words I don't want to use or to words that are weak or awkward, then they are doing me a disservice. I would rather take out rhyme and rhythm and use words that I really want. Usually there is a right word, and if you are led into using something that's second best, it's a great pity. To be true to the words that you want is most important of all.

JC: It is typical in your poetry to come to very short, uneven-in-length lines that slow the reader—that make the reader pause and linger over the descriptions as they unfold.

VW: Some of it is a matter of feeling and instinct where emphasis should fall. At other times, the words themselves dictate where they should be presented. Every word in a poem is important, and each should be placed as effectively as possible. It should always be where the emphasis seems best. It could be at the end of a line. A word could be given a line by itself for special emphasis. A line could build to a certain word. A word could be given emphasis in an uneven line. The fact that my lines are short gives greater importance to every word. Also, if you have a long line, then the line becomes more important than the individual words. With short lines, each word has to be the right word in exactly the right place. This puts a lot of pressure on me to get everything just right.

JC: You are considered by many to be the contemporary master of the lyric form. Have you ever thought of moving away from these "small poems" for a time in order to write some "incredibly huge poems" as well? Why not a rambling narrative once in a while?

VW: I just don't think it would work for me because of what I believe about the magic of the short line and the words being so important. In the sweep of narrative poetry, or at least with longer lines, the separate words get lost in the extended description. In my poetry I'm keeping everything very tightly focused, and this just would not work in a longer medium. I also like small things. I was small for my age as a child, and I always liked little things that could be contained, things that I could pick up in my hand and could see right in front of me. Somehow, the compression and self-contained quality of small things always appealed to me. I think this has gone along with my poems, too.

JC: Tell us about your work habits as a poet.

VW: I usually get an idea from something I've seen or thought about— an idea, image, phrase, or word that makes me feel that something should be done with it. Then I sit down and wrestle with it and try to get the words as true as I can to the subject. I work to get the right words, right sounds, and right images. In many cases I work on a very short poem for months. I have done hundreds of revisions for a single poem. Sometimes things work out almost immediately. It doesn't mean that one way is better than the other, or that one poem ends up being better than another. Some just work easily, and some are really difficult so that I have a great struggle getting them right. Some I never do get right. In fact, I have given up on some.

JC: How would you say you have changed most as a writer?

VW: Early on I wrote poetry not for children but for adults. The main change in me is that I shifted to writing for children because I liked the short form and the subject matter was still vivid from my own childhood. Along the way I discovered I was more suited to poetry for children. So many changes in taste and style take place in adult poetry; one has to worry constantly about what is fashionable and acceptable. But poetry for children deals with constants and universals. I find that very congenial and satisfying.

JC: How do you believe poetry should be shared with young readers?

VW: I would first encourage children to do what I did as a child, which is to read a lot of poetry—and not just poetry written for children. They should read poetry written for adults, too. This would give them a good balance between what's for fun and what is really serious and most true to the nature of poetry. They should also try writing poetry, because it can be enjoyable even if they don't go on to be poets. Writing poetry should be a great pleasure.

JC: What projects are next for you?

VW: I have two books of poetry still to be published. One is a book of Christmas poems. The other is a book of small poems, but it won't be called a "small poem" book. It will have a slightly different title, but the poems are pretty much the same. The only thing that is discouraging to me is that I have written about so many wonderful subjects, I now feel that I'm running out of things to write about. I'm going to take some time just to look around me and hope to come up with more subjects and inspirations. Then, perhaps, the poems will follow.

Select Bibliography

All the Small Poems (Farrar, Strauss, & Giroux, 1987).

Small Poems Again (Farrar, Strauss, & Giroux, 1986).

Still More Small Poems (Farrar, Strauss, & Giroux, 1978).

More Small Poems (Farrar, Strauss, & Giroux, 1976).

Small Poems (Farrar, Strauss, & Giroux, 1972).

Lee Bennett Hopkins

Lee Bennett Hopkins, poet and anthologist, is the Johnny Appleseed of contemporary children's poetry. He has spent his life spreading the virtues of poetry in classrooms, libraries, teacher workshops, and with parent groups. To date, he has published over thirty anthologies of poetry for children that range in subject matter from eating to reading to machines.

Hopkins believes that poetry time for the young should not be made an exercise in dissecting and analyzing. Rather, he feels that above all, children should be given the opportunity to develop an appreciation for and a true love for poetry. This can be accomplished in part, he believes, by making available to them different types of poems and giving them time to sample each.

To help give recognition to and celebrate the work of poets writing for children, Hopkins has recently endowed The Lee Bennett Hopkins Poetry Award, to be presented annually by the Children's Literature Council of Pennsylvania. The award will recognize the work of an American poet or compiler and will be given for an anthology of poetry or a collection of original poems for children published during the preceding year. Hopkins says of this award, "This is my own small way of giving back to the world of children's literature, a world which has been so wonderful to me."

Today, Lee Bennett Hopkins lives in Scarborough, New York.

Photo: Jeffrey Wein

JC: If one word represents your early life and career, it might be "contrasts." You went from living in the Seth Boyden Project in Newark, New Jersey, and being a disadvantaged child to a first teaching job in a sixth grade classroom in a modern, well-provisioned school in New Jersey, then back to working with disadvantaged children through programs you designed while teaching at Bank Street College in New York City. From these contrasts, how did you get started on your love affair with poetry?

LBH: This love affair really began while I was teaching in the 1960s. I always found that poetry was a wonderful vehicle for children, and in particular for slower readers, because poems are usually short, the vocabulary is usually simple, and I maintain that sometimes more can be said and felt in eight or ten or twelve lines than in an entire novel. There is great impact in poetry. I loved seeing this impact take hold in my students. When I was teaching, there really wasn't the range of poems we have available today, and through my work I am trying to add to this variety for all readers.

JC: Don't You Turn Back: Poems by Langston Hughes (1969) started you on your way to a lifetime as an anthologist. What would you say has been your greatest change as an anthologist since that first book?

LBH: As you grow and mature, you hope you get better at your craft, whether you're a plumber, sanitation worker, or whatever. I don't think my methods have changed that much, but I think my views have changed. I grew up in the city, and about eighteen years ago I moved to a very rural area here in Scarborough. The move and the new environment had a great influence on my work as a poet and as an anthologist. I went from being an asphalt kid to a nature kid. The environment here certainly has influenced a lot of the books I have done since I moved here.

JC: Tell us about your work habits as an anthologist.

LBH: I have a couple of methods I use when I'm working on a project. With an anthology, the first thing I do is to get a very good theme. Hopefully, it will be one that hasn't been explored to death. Then, I set out to read or reread all the poems I can related to this theme. I start literally from A to Z, from Adoff to Zolotow. Being in this business for so long, I know some poems well from a variety of sources, and there are poets I know who will have poems that will fit specific themes. I begin with the original sources, the original books of poetry. I try not to tap into other people's anthologies because I don't want a collection to be a collection of collections.

After I've explored A to Z, I have a group of people around the country whom I fondly call my "take-out" poets. I write to them and tell them what theme I'm working on. Often they respond with a wonderful poem that ends up in my collection. I solicit these poems for a few reasons. One, it gives them a chance to get published—it is very difficult to get poetry published in this country. Two, the new poems also give a freshness to my books. These authors bring forth poetry that teachers, librarians, and children have never read before. Many of these poets have a great deal of talent, but they might be having trouble getting their own books of poetry published. Hopefully—and this is what my aim is here—if they get enough published in anthologies and these poems are picked up, then one day they might grow into their own books. Above all, I believe in giving back and helping people.

JC: A characteristic of your anthologies is that you have a full range of poets, poetic forms, and time periods represented.

LBH: I always strive for a blend of old and new, in poets and in forms. I like to use the works of poets who have been writing for a long time, such as Aileen Fisher and David McCord. Their early work stands up as well today as it ever did. I think it is wonderful to acquaint readers, especially the younger audience, with their works and to give the readers a taste for the past, present, and hopefully the future as well. I want them to see the full range of beauty in poetry.

JC: You have worked with a number of illustrators when assembling your anthologies. How would you describe the typical relationship between the illustrator and the anthologist?

LBH: Most of the time in children's books, whether we are talking about poetry books or picture books, the writer and illustrator do not get together when working on the project. The coordination is usually the job of the editor at the publishing company. The editor has the task of finding an artist to match the book. I have been very lucky. I have done many books, and editors will often ask me my opinion of artists. In the case of *Side by Side* (1988), which is a large collection, the marriage was set up by Simon and Schuster. They wanted Hilary Knight and me to work together. They arranged for the two of us to have lunch one day to see if we might be compatible. It was love at first sight! Hilary and I now have a wonderful working relationship, but that sort of relationship is not always possible. There are many artists I have not met yet. Most of the time I see the art when readers see the art. Occasionally, a publisher will send me sketches, or they call me in for a meeting and we'll look at art, but even then I won't see all the finished art until the book is done.

JC: Your anthologies are not loaded down with the older, public domain poems, those that require no permission fees for publishing them. How have you managed to convince publishers to increase book budgets to allow you the freedom to choose more contemporary, and more expensive, poems?

LBH: It is a matter of philosophy. I don't want to include older works that have been used thousands of times before, pieces we all know and can recite. I just don't feel I need to use many of those. I would rather give new people a chance to be published. I'm doing books for the children of this and the next century. I don't need to dip back all that often into earlier centuries. I know my books cost a lot of money to produce, but I would rather pay the high fees and have a better book than fill them up with all that public domain poetry. There are good poems in the public domain; the point is that poems should not be used just *because* they are free for the using.

JC: What has been your most difficult task as an anthologist?

LBH: In many cases, the search for just the right type of poem for a collection has been a great challenge. I'm always surprised as to what is not out there. A lot of my books are theme books, like *To the Zoo* (1992) and *Dinosaurs* (1987). I thought about doing *Dinosaurs* for a long, long time. I imagined there were just scores of dinosaur poems out there, just like there had to be a plethora of poems about zoos. To my shock, I discovered there were very few dinosaur poems. *Dinosaurs* was in my files for ten years before it finally came to fruition. Then, the concept got in the way. I often get these wild ideas, and they won't leave my head. I decided that rather than doing a book of humorous poems about dinosaurs, I wanted to take a nonfiction approach. I wanted to trace both their evolution and extinction through the poetry. It was *very* difficult to find poems to fit that idea. Many of the poems in that book were commissioned from my take-out poets. Eight out of eighteen poems in the collection were brand new.

JC: After all the books you have assembled, what still makes a poem exciting for you?

LBH: It's the "oooh" factor. When I read a poem and say, "Oooh," then I know it's a good poem. I read poetry all the time, and I see every new book of poetry published each year for children and young adults. I have one of the most extensive libraries of poetry for children in the country. I read through all of the new books when they come out, and if I find a poem that makes me go, "Oooh," then I know it is one I'm going to use at some point. I still feel that if I like it, then children will like it, too.

JC: In *More Surprises* (1987), two of your own poems are included. One of these is "Good Books, Good Times!" Three years later you assembled the collection called *Good Books, Good Times!* (1990). The same poem also appears there. Repeating a poem from collection to collection is not something you usually do. Just how did that volume grow from this poem?

LBH: In 1985 the Children's Book Council asked me to be the poet for National Book Week. The theme that year was "Good Books, Good Times!" My charge was to write a verse based upon that slogan to fit on a bookmark! I included it in *More Surprises,* but I had been thinking about doing a book of poems about the joys of reading for a long time. That verse just sparked the idea for an entire collection.

JC: How would you like to see poetry and your anthologies shared with young readers?

LBH: Read poetry for the love and the fun of it—then leave it alone! Readers shouldn't be asked ridiculous questions about the poems— they shouldn't be beaten to death. We shouldn't worry about what this word means or that word means or what that phrase means or what the poet really meant. Just read the poem and love it. Children don't need to write a two-page essay about a poem in order to enjoy it. Read it and go on to something else. Poetry shouldn't be an exercise in dissecting, analyzing, and forced memorization.

It is wonderful when children write poetry, but it is often difficult for them to do because they haven't had much life experience. However, writing should be encouraged. They should also come to know that they can't be good writers until they are good readers, so they should read and be read to extensively. They have to hear words to get a feel for the language. Some adults feel that young children aren't very creative in their writings. We have to stop and think that these children can probably remember only three snowfalls! When I go into classrooms I do a lot with simile. I say to the children, "as green as . . . " They respond with "as green as grass." That is not a cliché to them. What is greener than grass to a six-year-old? They are just beginning to live. We get jaded as adults. We don't realize that their perceptions are normal and exciting to someone so young.

I once went on a field trip with a group of children who had just finished a unit about life on the farm. The teacher did a nice unit and had models of farm animals all around the classroom. As a culminating activity, we took a bus to a real farm. When we got off the bus, a little girl took one look at a cow standing nearby and went hysterical. I did not understand why until I took her aside and talked to her. She thought that the cow was going to be like the tiny little model that was in the classroom—that she could hold it in her hands. She never realized a cow could be so enormous. As adults we take too much for granted; we think children know everything. If a child is taken to the circus or zoo for the first time, whole new worlds open up for them. Those of us who work with young children should never forget that.

JC: Describe yourself as a poet.

LBH: I work hard. Very hard. I always tell children that if they want to write anything, they have to really work at it. Sometimes I don't think there is such a thing in this world as the word *writing*. There is only rewriting. Writing is easy. Rewriting is hard. We all have to realize that whatever we do in life will take a lot of practice, whether we are going to be a baseball player, a plumber, or an artist. I love what I do, but it is often very hard work.

JC: What do you think of the current state of poetry for children and young adults?

LBH: I think the world of poetry is in good shape. It is very exciting that the whole-language movement has us more aware of the importance of poetry. This movement has sparked a larger interest in poetry, an interest that has spread down to the children. There are also new poets coming along who are writing excellent works, such as J. Patrick Lewis, Constance Levy, and Deborah Chandra. There are new voices coming into poetry all the time; these will take us into the next century.

JC: What projects are next for you?

LBH: In the near future I will have a book of my own poems published. The third edition of *Let Them Be Themselves* (1992) has recently been republished, and I'm very excited about that. Two of my early novels have also been reissued by Simon and Schuster: *Mama* (1992) and *Mama and Her Boys* (1993), both of which relate my childhood years. I also have a compassionate collection of poems, *Through Our Eyes* (1992), poems relating to children living in the 1990s. Poems within that collection represent issues ranging from living in single-parent homes to the plight of the homeless. It is a very special volume to me.

I've been in this business a long time, but I'm still flabbergasted when I walk into a building where children know my work or I'll recite a poem and they will recite it with me. It's a wonderful feeling.

Select Bibliography

Anthologies Edited

Let Them Be Themselves (HarperCollins, 3rd edition, 1992).

Ring Out Wild Bells: Poems for Holidays and Seasons (Harcourt Brace Jovanovich, 1992).

Through Our Eyes (Little, Brown, 1992).

To the Zoo (Little, Brown, 1992).

Happy Birthday (Simon & Schuster, 1991).

On the Farm (Little, Brown, 1991).

Good Books, Good Times! (HarperCollins, 1990).

Still as a Star: Nighttime Poems (Little, Brown, 1989).

Side by Side: Poems to Read Together (Simon & Schuster, 1988).

Voyages: Poems by Walt Whitman (Harcourt Brace Jovanovich, 1988).

Click, Rumble, Roar: Poems about Machines (HarperCollins, 1987).

Dinosaurs (Harcourt Brace Jovanovich, 1987).

More Surprises (HarperCollins, 1987).

Pass the Poetry, Please! (HarperCollins, revised edition, 1987).

Creatures (Harcourt Brace Jovanovich, 1985).

Munching: Poems About Eating (Little, Brown, 1985).

The Sky Is Full of Song (HarperCollins, 1984).

Rainbows Are Made: Poems by Carl Sandburg (Harcourt Brace Jovanovich, 1982).

Morning, Noon, and Nighttime, Too (HarperCollins, 1980).

Don't You Turn Back: Poems by Langston Hughes (Alfred A. Knopf, 1969).

Novels

Mama and Her Boys (Simon & Schuster, 1993).

Mama (Simon & Schuster, 1992).

X. J. Kennedy

X. J. Kennedy's career as a writer began when he sold science fiction stories for a penny a word to pulp magazines. Since those days, Kennedy has become the writer many consider to be the master of nonsense verse for children and young adults. Such works as Ghastlies, Goops & Pincushions: Nonsense Verses *(1989) and* Brats *(1986) have delighted readers of all ages with their "harmless nonsense" and games.*

However, nonsense is not the only arena explored by Kennedy. A versatile writer, he also deals in his verse with such matters as being proud of one's own heritage, sex-role stereotyping, and family relationships. His greatest wish is to offer to young readers positive experiences with poetry so that he can "snatch children out of their cradles and take them through to the grave with poetry of one kind or another."

Kennedy lives with his wife, Dorothy, in Bedford, Massachusetts.

JC: Please tell us about the early influences upon you as a writer.

XJK: Well, I wasn't born into the kind of household where good children's books were abundant. My parents did read to me Robert Louis Stevenson's *A Child's Garden of Verses* and *Mother Goose,* but on my own I read mostly trash. I read comic books in great quantities, and when I got a little older, about thirteen or so, I discovered pulp magazines, then available in every drugstore. Science fiction especially captivated me. Other than a poem I wrote in the third grade which was seized by my teacher and printed in the local newspaper, I really didn't print much until after I discovered those science fiction magazines. I then would dash off letters to the editors. These were printed during World War II. Later, when I got to be about twenty-

Photo: Dorothy M. Kennedy

one, my first professional publications were a couple of science fiction stories in pulp magazines with names like *Other World* and *Science Fiction Quarterly.* I got a penny a word and was really proud! I had this notion that I'd become a science fiction writer like Asimov or Heinlein, but I soon realized that I wasn't prolific enough to make a living at it. I moved into teaching from there and taught for about twenty-five years. I guess I've come full-cycle now, because I'm back to writing full-time again.

JC: When did you make the decision to spend so much of your life writing, especially writing for younger readers?

XJK: I always liked to write and, as a kid, was always scribbling away like crazy. It was just natural to keep on scribbling. *Nude Descending a Staircase* (1961), a collection of poems for adults, was my first book. Writing for the younger crowd came later.

JC: You are considered one of the best writers of nonsense verse for children and young adults. Why have you chosen to excel in this area? Is there a connection between this type of verse and your views about sharing poetry with the young?

XJK: When kids first discover poetry of any sort, usually in school these days, it's the funny stuff they most enjoy. I would hope that nonsense verse might be a vehicle to win kids over to deeper poetry later. If they can tolerate nonsense verse first, they may go on to sample other types of poetry. I write nonsense verse just for the fun of it. I like the freedom to play around with sound effects, such as getting all kinds of words to rhyme inside of a line, like a bunch of bells inside a barrel.

JC: Hallmarks of your work include carefully measured metrics and the rich sound effects you mentioned. Through your work, the ear is tickled. Tell us how this comes about for you.

XJK: Well, nowadays I try to sit down early and work for most of the morning. Often I will start writing verse in bed when I wake up, all woozy and still involved with dreams. I tend to dawdle and compose verse with a sort of mental word processor. When you write in rhyme, as I do, it makes it easier to remember lines as they fall into place. You can play around and rewrite them, right there in your head. I can remember up to about twenty-four lines of verse before I write them down. Any more than that and my brain sloppeth over.

When I finally get out of bed and write them down, I use a word processor and rewrite a great deal. Writing with a computer enables me to fuss almost too long over the lines. When I revise, I am unconsciously looking for words to substitute for words that first occurred. I look for words to echo other words. For instance, this morning I was writing a limerick about a lady vampire:

> At each full moon, Aunt Draculeen Frump
> Dons her cape, takes a quick running jump

> And with fangs bared and twitchin'
> Flits out of the kitchen
> To return at dawn pleasingly plump.

In the first draft, I wrote:

> And with fangs bared and twitchin'
> Soars out of the kitchen

Then, when I looked it over I realized that *flits* would be better than *soars* because *flits* echoes *twitchin'* and also the *it* sound in *kitchen*. So *flits* was substituted there. That's the kind of change I'm always looking for.

I don't always find it possible to finish something immediately; inspiration will flag. I keep boxes full of fragments. I believe in keeping any loose lines of verse that occur to me like coins thrown into a beggar's bowl. I just hang on to them. Maybe at a later time, what couldn't be finished at one sitting will get going again.

JC: At times your work can be difficult to read for some readers because of this playfulness in language use. For example, "Sheepshape" (from *Ghastlies, Goops & Pincushions*) through alliteration becomes a wonderful tongue twister; it becomes a challenge for the reader. At other times, you create or arrange words differently through spelling or combining parts of words, seen in a poem like "Italian Noodles" (also from *Ghastlies, Goops & Pincushions*). Here you use such words as "Sloli," "Alretti," and "Fasta." What creative boundaries do you set for yourself when you write?

XJK: First of all, I would hope that readers would want to read the verses aloud so that the sound effects would be obvious. In "Italian Noodles," the made-up words are mere puns, used mainly because the pattern calls for a pun to end each stanza. I do observe certain "boundaries" when playing with the language: I'm always unwilling to invent a brand-new word. That is, I couldn't do like Dr. Seuss, whom I respected greatly. I couldn't make up a lot of words or funny names just because they rhymed. If I start doing that an alarm bell rings and a voice says, "Kennedy, you're cheating. Aren't there enough words in the English language as it stands? You don't need to make up any. You just need to work harder and find some that will rhyme with what you have." Language can be played with, but it should still have a root in the reality of things.

JC: Fresh Brats (1990) and *Brats* contain some of the silliest, most ridiculous, most mischievous characters in all of contemporary poetry written for children and young adults. The creation of these sorts of characters is another hallmark of your work. Tell us about the origins of these collections.

XJK: A brats poem is a playful game, one that follows certain ironbound rules. I was inspired by the "Little Willie" poems of the turn of the century. People like Harry Graham and other light verse poets wrote these things for adults. You'll find Little Willies in earlier anthologies. Little Willie was a brat who always got the fate he deserved, as in this anonymous example:

> Little Willie from his mirror
>   Licked the mercury all off,
> Thinking, in his childish error,
>   It would cure the whooping cough.
>
> At the funeral his mother
>   Brightly said to Mrs. Brown,
> " 'Twas a chilly day for Willie
>   When the mercury went down."

That sort of thing. When I'm making up a brats poem, I am trying to tell a complete story in a very short space. It may be four lines, six lines, or eight lines—all ending with a surprise or some sort of verbal magic trick in the last line. It also has to have a very strict form, a tight rhyme scheme. These are the rules of the game for me.

JC: In your work you cover a wide range of subjects and types of poems. In addition to the silly, you also explore a more serious, sometimes darker side of life, a side that surprises many of the readers of your light verse. Readers come across such poems as "Louleen's Feelings" (being proud of one's own heritage) and "The Girl Who Makes Cymbals Bang" (examining sex-role stereotyping), both from *The Kite That Braved Old Orchard Beach* (1991).

XJK: Readers will see more realistic stuff from me in the future. It's easy for me to shift from one type to the other, because I've had a chronic inability to distinguish between so-called serious poetry and so-called light verse. I don't know quite where to draw the line between the serious and the frivolous. In poems I have written for adults, there's humor mixed in with the seriousness. I've done a fair amount of "serious" verse for kids. Out of nine collections for kids, six of them are nonsense verse, and three might be called realistic or serious. I also have a book coming out called *The Beasts of Bethlehem.* It is a series of little poems purportedly spoken by various creatures who were present at the Nativity. So, the seriousness is an important part of my work, too. I don't always try for laughs.

JC: Does this serious emphasis signal a change in philosophy or style for you? Are we seeing an evolution of sorts here?

XJK: Probably not. In my poems for adults I haven't changed much at all. I've stood pat and haven't learned a thing over the last thirty-five years. Some people say that a poet has to learn new tricks, has to be a shifting, changing chameleon who goes on developing. Some poets do that; others don't. Emily Dickinson didn't change all that much from beginning to end. She always favored the little hymn-like stanzas. I don't think writers always have to change; if they can hang on to what they've got, that's enough to be thankful for.

My writing for children didn't really start until about 1974 when I was encouraged by Myra Cohn Livingston, who showed a couple of children's poems I had published in that first adult book, *Nude Descending a Staircase,* to Margaret McElderry, a wonderful editor. Ms. McElderry then wrote and asked me for a whole collection of poems for children. I was very much encouraged and sustained by her kind support. It is largely because of her that I have gone on writing children's verse.

JC: What would you say have been the most important changes in poetry for children and young adults that you have seen since you began writing for children?

XJK: Some say that we are now in the middle of a renaissance of poetry for children. There is plenty of evidence to support that view. The popularity of anthologies has shown booksellers that children's poetry is not poison at the box office; quite the contrary. Of course, the read-aloud movement and the California Reading Initiative have caused more poetry for children to appear in elementary school readers these days. I am delighted by this.

I believe, looking back over children's poetry for the past fifty years, that there has been a great development in antisweetness, a sort of irreverent realism less seldom seen fifty years ago. If one goes back to older anthologies for children from the 1920s, one finds that most of the stuff is awfully sweet, almost cloying. The view of childhood is romantic and tends to cast a gloss of pleasant antirealism over everything. All that changed when people like John Ciardi got writing. I think Ciardi had an immense influence. Even in his nonsense verse, he shows that children are at times dirty and highly emotional creatures. He made it possible for the rest of us to carry on; he poked a pin in the old notion that children are always angels, that their world is all cookies and cream. Ciardi reminded us that childhood has its traumas and shocks and its insults. He did a great deal to shape our present view of what poetry for children can be, and he really paved the road for writers like me.

JC: How would you like teachers and others who work with young readers to introduce your poetry to the young?

XJK: With zeal. Seriously, I'd be grateful to anyone who might read my stuff aloud. That is one of the best ways to get children to care for poetry. Read it with some attention to the sound effects. You can ham it up with an audience of kids—even if one is not a professional actor. Turn on the histrionics and have a ball! *Ghastlies, Goops & Pincushions,* to mention one book, has a great deal of comic stuff in it, possibly appealing to kids newly arrived to poetry. I hope.

JC: You are also considered to be an outstanding anthologist. *Knock at a Star: A Child's Introduction to Poetry* (1982) was your first venture into this area. Tell us about your beliefs and feelings related to your work as an anthologist.

XJK: Knock at a Star was a collaboration with my wife, Dorothy. We wanted to do a book to put poetry right into kids' hands. That is, we wanted to do a book that would not have to be read to kids but one that younger readers might read for themselves. In doing that book we went against much received wisdom. When we read what experts had said about children's poetry, we kept running into the familiar refrain, "Poetry should not be analyzed. Children can't take analysis of poetry." We questioned that. It seemed to Dorothy and me that children enjoy looking at things close up. They like to see how a machine works, like to see an animal at close range. If they like to inspect things closely and see how they work, why could children not apply this curiosity to poetry?

In a way, the idea for *Knock at a Star* grew out of a college textbook. I've been the editor of a book called *An Introduction to Poetry,* which first came out in 1968, and for which an eighth edition is now in the works. That book analyzes poetry by breaking poems down into their elements. That has always seemed to me to be a very good way to teach poetry, because the human mind cannot always grasp a whole poem at once. If a student looks at one particular element, say the sound of a poem or its imagery or vocabulary or the story it tells, he or she may more readily begin to understand what is going on in a complicated poem. *Knock at a Star* breaks poetry down into various elements and illustrates these elements with poems. This is exactly the same method I used in the college textbook. As far as we've been able to tell, from all accounts received, kids of eight to twelve respond well to this approach.

We had one other wish in putting together *Knock at a Star.* When we looked at older anthologies, we found them heavy on poems by great poets of the English canon, poets who, not incidentally, are safely out of copyright, poets like Shakespeare and Shelley. Therefore, their works require no permission fees and are free for use in anthologies. Our conviction was that any American child we knew would be unlikely to stand still for Shelley's "Ode to the West Wind" or Shakespeare's deathless sonnets. These are poems I revere myself and would hope children could grow up to. But in *Knock at a Star,* we were determined to put poems we thought would immediately appeal to actual children we knew, our own five children and others. We tried to make the poems short, cheerful, and interesting in some way or other. That was really the rationale in back of the book and is my philosophy as a children's anthologist. My ambition is to reach children early on and get them to care for poetry. I would love to snatch children out of their cradles and take them through to the grave with poetry of one kind or another.

JC: What projects are next for you?

XJK: Dorothy and I put together a new anthology for pre-readers, *Talking Like the Rain,* which has just been published. *The Beasts of Bethlehem* will be out soon. Also coming up is a new book of poems for adults, *Dark Horses.* I've just taken a column for the *Harvard Review,* so I'll be busy with that. I also foresee a sequel to the only novel I've written for children, *The Owlstone Crown,* which is a fantasy story that takes place in a land dominated by a colossal moonflower. I really think that is the best thing I have written in my life. Down the line, I hope, there will be more verse for children, both realistic and nonsensical. I'll keep busy.

Select Bibliography

The Beasts of Bethlehem (McElderry/Macmillan, 1992).

The Kite That Braved Old Orchard Beach: Year-Round Poems for Young People (McElderry/Macmillan, 1991).

Fresh Brats (McElderry/Macmillan, 1990).

Ghastlies, Goops & Pincushions: Nonsense Verses (McElderry/Macmillan, 1989).

Brats (McElderry/Atheneum, 1986).

Cross Ties: Selected Poems (University of Georgia Press, 1985).

The Forgetful Wishing Well: Poems for Young People (McElderry/Macmillan, 1985).

Anthologies Edited

Talking Like the Rain: A Read-to-Me Book of Poems, with Dorothy M. Kennedy (Little, Brown, 1992).

Knock at a Star: A Child's Introduction to Poetry, with Dorothy M. Kennedy (Little, Brown, 1982).

Books about Poetry

An Introduction to Poetry (HarperCollins, 7th edition, 1990).

Gary Soto

As a youngster, Gary Soto was a "playground kid" who spent his days playing kickball and dodgeball. Academics held very little interest for him until he discovered such Beat poets as Lawrence Ferlinghetti and Allen Ginsberg; it wasn't long before he traded his dodgeball for a pen. He started writing poetry while in his early twenties and has since published several volumes for young readers, including the highly acclaimed Fire in My Hands *(1990).*

Soto believes that before younger readers attempt to write serious poetry, they should spend their days reading all types of poetry and gathering what he calls "working life" experiences, those that might later become subjects for poems. Recently, he has become a producer/distributor of films for the younger audience. He is also a master storyteller who enthralls children during his visits to the schools.

Gary Soto lives today in Berkeley, California.

JC: What was Gary Soto like as a youngster, and which events would you say most shaped you as a writer?

GS: I grew up in Fresno, California, on a poor street, and there weren't a lot of things in the house. This, perhaps, prompted a deeper experience, a deeper living and thinking on my part. We were a working-class family, and my family situation wasn't entirely happy. As a result, today I tell children that no matter what kind of dire straits they may find themselves in at a young age, there is always a chance to improve life and make something of the mind and body.

Photo: Carolyn Soto

I really wasn't a good student in school. I was what you might call a "playground kid." I enjoyed playing games, all types of games: dodgeball, kickball, football, soccer. I wasn't interested in studying at all. I was a fighter on occasion, a rambunctious kid with a few tricks up my sleeve. I finally woke up when I was about twenty years old. This was after about two years of being in City College in Fresno. I became interested in writing poetry after I discovered a few of the Beat poets, like Ferlinghetti, Corso, and Ginsberg. I was fascinated by what they could say in the writing. I wanted to do the same thing after I had read their poetry. It was just a total illumination for me. Ferlinghetti was a good poet for me to sink my teeth into. He was a powerful figure to someone who was young and impressionable.

JC: From this interest, how did your first published pieces come about?

GS: I sent off everything I could to literary magazines, the same ones my teachers followed. I felt I should follow the same course and try to get published where they were getting published. I sent poems to *Paris Review, The Nation, Poetry*—magazines that had the stature and importance in American literature. Eventually, something was accepted, and I went from there.

JC: Do you have suggestions for younger students who are now writing poetry and hope to submit it to various publishers?

GS: First, I would try to find a teacher to guide your poetry writing. Some teachers will save you time, and you need to make the effort to seek them out. In terms of publication, I really don't recommend that younger people—those under twenty—send poetry to magazines. It is very rare for a person to get published at a young age. Historically, poets don't mature until they reach their mid-twenties or older. When you are younger, write first to please yourself. Practice, practice, practice. Write to express your own world and its inhabitants.

In *A Fire in My Hands*, I talk about young poets, young writers needing to look into their own lives for material. I call this "working life." I know it is hard for many who are young to see that there is value in their lives, that there are moments in their lives that are worth reporting through writings. In many ways it is like gossip or storytelling around the table. If they can take one little slice of life and be able to focus on that piece, that makes for the better poem. That is what I do. What I usually find with younger writers is that they write so generally, write so widely that they don't communicate to the reader. What we like to hear are the really intimate details of all our lives. If younger writers could just adjust their focus from this wide-lens view to a focused-lens view, the writings would be powerful.

JC: A Fire in My Hands is quite different from what young readers typically find in a poetry collection. Here, you have both introductory comments for poems and a "Question and Answer" section at the end of the book. What were your reasons for using this particular structure?

GS: The book was shaped by an editor at Scholastic. I liked her suggestions and ideas about format very much. I put questions and answers toward the back of the book and sprinkled little anecdotes that would introduce each of the poems as they appeared. Teachers seem to be fascinated by the questions and the answers. If it helps them and the students better understand the poetry, then so much the better.

JC: In this "Question and Answer" section, you say that you once worked on a fourteen-line poem for an entire week. Please expand upon this by sharing with us your own process of composing.

GS: First, I drink a lot of coffee to get me going! I usually write in the morning. I try to write as quickly as possible, both my prose and poetry. If I work on a book of poems, I try to get eight or nine poems written really quickly so I can see a book taking shape. That direction is very important to me. What I like doing is completing books, whether they be prose or poetry books. I hate writing them. That is, I hate working for days on end. Completing them is the fun part for me. It is nice at the end of all that work actually to see something happening.

Once in a while I also lift weights out in the backyard to clear and focus my mind when I am writing on a project. It helps kill the boredom of having to sit at the computer all day. I have adapted to computer, but I really like to write my poetry on a typewriter. I like seeing it appear on paper, and I like putting handwritten comments between the lines before typing it again. Some friends of mine think I'm crazy, but I really miss that when I compose on computer. There is just something special about typing out a portion of a poem, maybe four or five lines, and ripping it out of the carriage, looking at it, and adding handwritten material.

I also try to put time lines on what I do. I'm actually quite "antsy" about completing projects. Sometimes I admit this doesn't make for the best writing, but that's my writing habit. My writings occur because I do use deadlines. Otherwise, I would procrastinate away. After I set this deadline, I work consistently until I wrap it up.

JC: How do you hope your younger readers respond to your writings?

GS: I get my share of letters from readers, and these letters usually have to do with a kinship between their experiences and my experiences, at least the ones described in my stories and poems. It's not all autobiographical. They say they see themselves in my stories, and this pleases me greatly. If they see this kinship, then I'm satisfied.

JC: Your poetry, as a rule, does not make use of regular rhythm and rhyme. Rather, the poems are held together through a variety of other structural devices.

GS: My own coming of age as a poet led to this. I studied and admired poets who were not using rhyme and meter. What I followed as a reader of poetry is what I took to be a "truth." I grew up reading poets who had very classical training, poets like James Wright and Galway Kinnell and Phillip Levine. They wrote at first in rhyme and meter but fell away from it as they grew as writers. Today, I can say I am fashioning my own poetry as a result of the poets who came before me and influenced me. It might be interesting for younger readers to read some Galway Kinnell and see if they notice similarities between his work and mine.

JC: It is also most typical for a reader of your work to find a detailed narrative. These narratives are gardens of imagery, storehouses of details.

GS: The narratives reflect the way I look at the world most of the time. I love telling stories. As a result, a good many of my poems have a narrative structure or base to them. There is a story, either mine or someone else's, to tie all together. A narrative structure links people.

JC: In terms of structure, your poetry, like much of Pablo Neruda's, gathers its power and strength through the short, tight line.

GS: By training, by appreciation, I am an imagist, one who tries to provide a really stark, quick image. I feel that a leaner poem is a better poem. The verbiage that some poems have is really boring to me. Pablo Neruda is one of my favorite poets. I really admire what he does in his work, both imagistically and in terms of the passion and romance in his writing. I'm sure his work has had a great influence on me as a writer. I look at his poems and say, "What a writer!"

JC: The range of subjects and emotions in *Neighborhood Odes* (1992) is quite remarkable: from a goat that steals a pipe to weight lifting. The "ode" seems to be a natural match to you, and the form allows you to move into so many subjects.

GS: From the beginning, I had younger readers in mind as the audience for this collection. I wanted to start with the praises of everyday life, beginning with things that are typically right in front of us: a sprinkler, or a place down the street. I enjoyed writing this one quite a bit. The word "odes" comes from Pablo Neruda's own odes, his elemental odes. I have great respect for those.

JC: Choose one of your poems you feel best represents your work as a poet and share with us how you feel it does this.

GS: One of the happiest poems, to me, I have written is called "Hitchhiking with a Friend and a Book That Explains the Pacific Ocean," which is now in *A Fire in My Hands*. What I was trying to do in this poem was capture a moment with another friend; his name is also Gary. He and I were hitchhiking toward the coast, and there was an incredible clarity to the day. At that moment, I just thought the experience was something like Zen. We were on the side of a road looking around, and everything was absolutely, stunningly clear and beautiful. It was a very happy moment in my life. It is probably a very minor poem in all the poems I have written, but it was special for me to be able to recreate that moment on the page. It is one of the healthiest poems I have written. The poem is also special because this is that "working life" I mentioned earlier. Where possible, the lines should come from one's own direct observations and experiences.

JC: Tell us about your work with younger readers in the schools.

GS: I've been doing more and more of that lately. When I visit schools, it isn't just to read poetry. I also read my stories and do a fair amount of storytelling. I really enjoy the storytelling above all. I have also done two films, so I share those films with young people when possible. The films are called *The Bike* and *The Pool Party*. *The Bike* is the story of a boy on his first bicycle and how he used it to begin an odyssey around his neighborhood. It is a short film: eleven minutes long. I was really pleased when it was named one of the top nine videos of 1992 by *School Library Journal*. *The Pool Party* is a half-hour film that will appear on independent television stations within the next few years. It is about a boy who gets invited to a wealthy girl's Saturday swim. He's a poor boy; she's a rich girl. It is a film of class difference, not racial difference.

JC: Do you have a special message you would like to send along to your readers?

GS: As you march along in life, reading is one of the best habits you can acquire to widen the mind and make it grow. It is a shame that for many kids between the ages of ten to eighteen, reading time begins to diminish. Reading is a beautiful passion. Stay with it always.

Also, be selective in your reading. Leave the boundaries of this country and read as widely as possible. Read literature by European writers, Latin American writers, African writers, Asian writers. It is really exciting to think about what others are doing in different countries at the same time.

If I could change anything about our reading habits, in particular I wish we could have more Mexican American writers easily accessible for younger readers. It is a shame we do not have more of their work in books used in the schools. That needs to change. And finally, read my prose, too!

Select Bibliography

Neighborhood Odes (Harcourt Brace Jovanovich, 1992).

Pacific Crossing (Harcourt Brace Jovanovich, 1992).

The Shirt (Delacorte, 1992).

Baseball in April & Other Stories (Harcourt Brace Jovanovich, 1991).

Taking Sides (Harcourt Brace Jovanovich, 1991).

A Fire in My Hands (Scholastic, 1990).

Eloise Greenfield

Eloise Greenfield's writings are enriched by the presence of a dual family: the family within and the family of all people. Within these circles, the reader meets strong characters who give power and life to the lines. They are also reflections of her own family ties: Greenfield grew up in a home where the arts were cherished, and her mother, Lessie Jones Little, was a gifted writer herself.

Greenfield has strong beliefs about sharing literature with the young. Particularly, she believes that the works of all peoples must be given equal attention in the schools, as opposed to having just one section of the reading curriculum devoted to "multicultural" selections. This equal sharing of all viewpoints in the literature will then help foster in children a true love for and excitement for language.

Greenfield creates her characters in Washington, D.C.

JC: Night on Neighborhood Street (1991) is a showcase for one of the hallmarks of your writing: the importance of family. Here, we not only see life within families such as those of Juma's and the Robinsons', but we also experience the family of the neighborhood. In your work and through your work, the reader is ever conscious of this duality.

EG: Family has always been very important to me personally. When I write, it *always* finds its way into my work. It does have to do with that duality of not just blood relatives but the family wherever it appears. This could be in a neighborhood or a church or support groups. Wherever people are willing to care about each other, support each other, and there is give and take, we have a family. I do like to write about that a lot because it does exist. That is very important to me.

I'm trying mostly to reflect the lives that African American children know they lead. These lives are not very much depicted by the media. What I want to do is give a balanced view of life and of family life, which will include negative but also positive aspects. In general, I think we see just the negative. This needs to change. This must change.

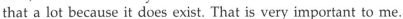

JC: Another hallmark of your work related to this depiction of the family is that you create some of the most powerful, vivid characters in all of poetry being written for the young.

EG: Thank you. If this happens, it's because the people I see are wonderful. I create from real-life composites of real people. Ever since I was a child I've always spent a lot of time observing people, just trying to figure out who they are. I think all children do this. As we get older, we don't do it as much, but writers have to. Human behavior and human personality are complex, so to avoid stereotyping it is necessary to look beneath the surface and see the *whole* person. That's what I try to do not only in observing people but also in creating characters. I try to create whole people as much as the space will allow for the work that's being written. Writers focus themselves so that some focus on nature or various other themes, and it is valid to focus where your interests are. I'm not saying that people who focus on nature don't care about people at all. What I am saying is that people should write about what they are drawn to; I happen to be drawn most to people. People are most important of all to me.

I would also like to see more variety in African American children's literature. Many of the African Americans who exist in real life are not being portrayed in books.

JC: In your writing, a heavy-handed message does not slap the reader in the face, but messages are nonetheless quite clear: Stay away from the drug pusher, unemployment hits hardest in families, family ties are to be cherished, and so on.

EG: In adult literature, the viewpoint of the author is more deeply hidden in metaphors and symbolic language than it is in children's literature. There are many things I want to say to children, but they are not primarily for instruction. For example, I think of "Nerissa," which is in *Night on Neighborhood Street.* In this poem I wanted to give a portrait of a child whose family is having problems. The father is unemployed and the mother is sick. The child wants to help. That's all. I really didn't have a message other than that. It was a reflection of this child who exists in many families. This character wants to help because she sees her parents suffering and wants to do something to make them feel better. It is not instruction for the reader. It is the real world, a world all of us should know about and care about. I hope readers identify with the characters and have a deeper understanding of the situation. I try to give the kind of interpretation that is more like a painting than a snapshot.

JC: For you, then, what would be the best interaction between reader and print?

EG: I want to enhance the love children have for language. They all have it, because they love jokes and riddles and stories. I want to build upon that. I want to create an excitement about literature, about ideas, about life, and help them develop strong appreciation for themselves.

JC: Tell us about your own process of composing.

EG: I try to write every day, but there are periods when I don't, periods during which other work becomes overwhelming or there are family responsibilities. But, in general, I try to write every day. My favorite time to write is from midnight to about four or five in the morning. In order to do that I take a nap during the day. I love the quiet of the night and the feeling of isolation. It is a time when I can just shut off all other thoughts and go to the place I need to go in order to see these people that I see.

I begin in longhand, but I've also found that I can start on the word processor, which was a pleasant surprise. I always write many drafts and continue to revise until I am perfectly happy with the piece—or at least as happy as I think I can be and feel I have done my best work.

JC: Please lead us through the writing of one of your poems to amplify these ideas.

EG: "Nathaniel's Rap" was written because I was fascinated by the form of rap, which is a form of poetry as valid as any other of the traditional forms. I wanted to write a rap poem. I finally decided to write a poem about a boy I named Nathaniel. I didn't know him well, because this was going to be just one poem. However, after I had written just a few lines, he became so real to me that I knew I wanted to do a whole book rather than just that one poem. That's the way *Nathaniel Talking* (1989) came about.

My next step was to try to think about some of the other aspects of Nathaniel's life. Each time I would finish one poem, I would spend a lot of time thinking about what else Nathaniel might want to talk about, what else was on his mind. I wrote of his feelings about his family, his future, his desire for knowledge, and his mistakes as well.

JC: Tell us about your own birth as a writer. What early influences most shaped your writing?

EG: Both of my parents loved the arts, so we were surrounded by that.

We went to the theater, jazz shows, operas. I studied piano. We also went to the library every week and got armloads of books. Listening to the radio was also an important constant in my family. All these were just normal parts of my childhood. My mother liked to draw, and she wrote a couple of songs. She also liked to rehearse children for plays and put on programs and fashion shows with children in the neighborhood. My interest in writing was greatly influenced by my parents and their love of the arts.

JC: Your mother, Lessie J. Little, was a writer of great talent. Her poems in *Children of Long Ago* (1988), like your own poems, are especially warm and inviting.

EG: She began writing after I did, actually. When I was little, Mother was helping us put on plays, writing songs, helping with performances in church, but everything was just around the house, so to speak. It was not anything on a professional level. She told me she had once written a story, sent it out, and had it rejected. Because of that experience, she had never written another story. After I began writing and getting published, she became interested again and began writing in her late sixties. *Children of Long Ago* was very special to my family because, although my mother knew it was being published and was very excited about the fact that it had been accepted, she did not live to see the completed book.

JC: Under the Sunday Tree (1988) presents another undercurrent found within your work: One should always be proud of one's heritage.

EG: Again, I intended no specific message or instruction here, but each reader brings something different, a different interpretation, to any piece of literature. This book was done in the reverse of the usual order: The paintings were done first. Then, an editor at Harper and Row asked me if I'd be interested in writing poetry to accompany Amos Ferguson's paintings. He is a Bahamian who lives in and paints the life in and around Nassau. I have never been there, but I had his original paintings at my home. I would set one up and study it carefully for several days to see what the artist had said. That's how those poems were developed. I did some reading about the Bahamas and did talk to my brother, who goes there often, but really everything was in those paintings.

My feeling about being proud of one's heritage is that if African American children know the truth about their heritage, they will automatically be proud. We don't really have to tell them to be proud; we just have to tell them what the truth is.

Mr. Ferguson did a wonderful painting of three Bahamians carrying objects on their heads, and this became the poem "Tradition." I wanted to show the history, the African origin, of this custom. That's why I mention Africa there. What I tried to do in this book was give a portrait of the Bahamas that was in keeping with what Amos Ferguson had done.

JC: The poem "Her Dreams" in this collection shows a young person reaching for jeweled moments in life: goals and dreams that are real but also require great effort to attain. These dreams are also strong undercurrents in your work.

EG: In this poem I wanted to write about the fact that we do have to reach for these moments, and they are not just goals. Any moment that brings us joy is important. It can be a few minutes or a month or a year. This is the joy that punctuates our entire lives, punctuates all the tragedies and pain. Several years ago, a friend of my mother said to her, "It has been a joyous journey." The reason she could say this—because I know she had pain, too—was that she was thinking of all of those moments that make life worthwhile. These are moments I like to talk about in my poetry. Many dreams are realized; some are not. Both need to be shared. We need to know that many of them are attainable, but we have to reach for them.

JC: This undercurrent of dreams is also the focus of *Daydreamers* (1981). How have younger readers with whom you have worked responded to the ideas in this collection?

EG: This is a collection I have used more often with small groups. I like to talk with children in a classroom rather than in an auditorium because the children and I can have a more thoughtful discussion in the quiet setting. What I have usually done is ask them to talk about their daydreams and let them know that daydreaming is an important growth period and not a waste of time.

I received a wonderful letter from a child who was in fourth grade. She said that she enjoyed the book but didn't understand all of it at first. She then said, "After I thought about it, I knew that it was about me." The reason I remember that letter is that it was so special to me that she had had that experience.

JC: Tell us about your work with younger readers in the schools.

EG: Several times I have applied for teaching grants from the Washington, D.C. Commission on the Arts and Humanities, which is our local arm of the National Endowment for the Arts. I've had three of these grants, and I have taught creative writing in the schools to children in grades four through six. I have done that three different semesters. Those were all very enjoyable experiences. I focused on characterization because I feel that is an area where many children are weak in their writings. I wanted them to bring characters to life. Many of them were already very good at telling a story in sequence, especially in action stories, but I wanted them to focus on people, to look inside characters, to do character sketches and put these characters in stories.

When I visit schools on my own, I do a more literary type of program rather than creative writing. However, it is hard for me to get my own writing done when I'm going back and forth between the schools, so I've decided I'm going to take a couple of years off and devote my time to writing.

JC: While you are on this sabbatical, how would you like to see your poetry shared in the schools?

EG: As I meet teachers from around the country at conferences, I see that they are pretty much doing what I would want them to do, that is, to try to give that excitement about language. They teach about the craft of poetry. They talk about the experiences that the characters have and encourage the children to relate similar experiences they've had or someone they know has had. They also have children memorize the poems that lend themselves to oral presentation and recite them and dramatize them, often in speech choirs. The poems are also used to inspire the children to write, after a discussion of the craft. I am pleased to see all of this going on; I hope it continues.

JC: What is next for you in your writing?

EG: Two books will be published shortly, an alphabet book and a counting book which Jan Spivey Gilchrist and I have done together. Next year will see the publication of another picture book. Beyond that, I have several projects that I'd like to do. I want to write another novel for young children and more picture books. At some point I'd even like to do some short stories for adults.

JC: Is there a special message you'd like to send along to your readers?

EG: I'd like to tell them to keep thinking and to take care of themselves. Remember that those of us who are writing, although we can't always visit schools because there aren't enough of us to go around, come to them through our work, and we really do care about them.

I'd also like to say a little more about my overall philosophy. When a book is completed, it does not just take its place in libraries and schools and homes. It becomes a part of the total environment. Every book that is published moves out into the environment and takes its place, for good or not so good. I keep that in mind as I'm revising a manuscript: What effect will this book have on the environment? Am I writing a book that will perpetuate the stereotypes and negative images, or am I writing a book that will help us balance the environment, make it a healthier place for children to live? I hope that in that way I can make a contribution.

I also have a comment about multiculturalism, about the literature being published in the United States. I think we have to divide the entire pie evenly, and not just give one slice of the pie to "multicultural literature," so that people of color aren't squeezed into one little corner. Each group should be fully represented; it's important that all of our voices are heard.

Select Bibliography

Night on Neighborhood Street (Dial Books, 1991).

Nathaniel Talking (Black Butterfly Children's Books, 1989).

Under the Sunday Tree (HarperCollins, 1988).

Daydreamers (Dial Books, 1981).

Childtimes: A Three-Generation Memoir, with Lessie Jones Little (Thomas Y. Crowell, 1979).

Honey, I Love and Other Love Poems (Thomas Y. Crowell, 1978).

Barbara Juster Esbensen

It may be that Barbara Juster Esbensen creates the most striking, vivid, and refreshing (and at times downright unusual) images of all those writing today for children and young adults. While the messages and thoughts found within her poems are challenging and represent a full range of concerns of the young, it is the skillful layering of images that creates the magic in each. The reader can alternately be touched by the closing of the year in "December Hills," be awed by bursts of color in "Fourth of July," and be held spellbound by the eeriness of "A Halloween Ghost Story" (from Cold Stars and Fireflies, 1984). *In her poetry, just when the reader feels relaxed enough to skitter through the lines, an unexpected and perfectly extraordinary image will startle the reader into new manners of thinking about the subject at hand. Reading each poem becomes an adventure to discover the beauty within each of her unique perceptions.*

Esbensen weaves her images in Edina, Minnesota.

Photo: Daniel M. Esbensen

JC: One of your greatest gifts as a poet is your ability to see the world through fresh images. A collection like *Cold Stars and Fireflies,* for example, could have been a disaster in the hands of a less-skilled poet, one who would have emphasized the old clichés of the seasons. Instead, you present such interesting and surprising images as leaves compared to coins raining down in "Questions for September" and the wind's whirling skirt hem in "Wooly Bear Caterpillar." Just what is it about you and how you view the world that brings you to these beautiful and different impressions?

BJE: I know that I'm a noticer, and all of my life I have thought of things that remind me of other things. I can remember when I was in ninth grade—my dad was a musician and my mother a singer—we used to spend a lot of time just sitting quietly and listening to music. I remember once listening to a Benny Goodman recording of Mozart's "Clarinet Quintet." The way the clarinet notes sounded one after the other just reminded me of a series of rounded pearls dropping one by one off a broken strand into water. I think I've always thought like that. And you bring up the whirling skirt image; I can remember what I was thinking when I wrote that: I was picturing leaves swirling up under feet as you walk along, and then having an image of a skirt hem doing that—you know, an old-fashioned skirt making the leaves move. I guess I've just always seen those images.

JC: In this collection, the reader is also guided through a delicate balance of personification, simile, and metaphor in the poems, a balance that is a trademark of your work. When you write, do you consciously begin with one of these elements and build from there, or do you begin with the images and work to these elements? Inside out, or outside in?

BJE: I suppose it's different with each poem. In the poem "Cardinal" (from *Cold Star and Fireflies*), I thought of the cardinal as a splash of paint first. I mean, I was just thinking of it as a splash on the white landscape, but paint wasn't right in that poem. Then I thought of a Chinese-chop, the mark the Chinese put at the bottom of a painting. It is often in red ink, so that got me to the word ink instead of paint. The whole thing then seemed like a Chinese poem to me. Really, sometimes I do begin with a simile and build from there, and other times I work just the opposite while writing. But I *do* think in terms of simile.

Sometimes I just sit and scribble things on a piece of paper to get my brain going, and many times in that process something occurs to me that I put someplace else in the poem. Then after I do a couple of rough drafts, I realize that such and such can start the poem, so it isn't always that my brain started them that way. I save my rough drafts of some poems, and they are really a mess. The way I'm thinking is so far in precision from what the final poem is. I used to throw all these drafts away, but the Kerlan Collection at the University of Minnesota wants everything now, so I save them. I used to throw away everything as soon as I did something better on the next page. I never wanted to see those drafts again! I've saved them since *Cold Stars and Fireflies*, and that's useful when I go out and talk to children. When kids ask about my writing process, I can show them that sometimes a poem starts with none of this good stuff. I can show them thirty pages of scratches and then the three pages that worked out the way I wanted. It shows them we all need to write, write, and then write some more before we end up with the best we can do.

JC: A technical aspect of your poetry that makes it very different is that aside from the dash, you use very little punctuation within the lines. It is also interesting that a complete thought never follows the dash; what follows is an amplifying phrase, most often an absolute construction. A few examples from *Cold Stars:*

In "Cardinal": "—a feathered ending to a poem about snow" (describing the cardinal).

In "Flyway": "—a heavy ribbon spiraling into corn rows" (describing geese flying).

In "Storm": "—a fist in the mouth!" (describing the rain).

BJE: I didn't know I did that so regularly. That's very interesting. I think most authors don't know they've done that kind of stuff. I prefer to use double spaces instead of periods, semicolons, and the like. The double spaces make the reader stop and take a breath. Like in "Mittens." It says in this poem that they "practice the piano—fiddle with the TV," and I wanted fiddle to be out there next to piano to create the wordplay. I just thought it was funny. I like the *look* of the dash or space on the page. I think it stops a reader more than a comma. After a comma the reader kind of rushes on. But there is just something about a dash—a horizontal line—that makes one stop a little more.

JC: This is a relatively new feature in your work. The spacing and use of the dash weren't used very much in your earlier work.

BJE: In earlier works like *Swing Around the Sun* (1965), I was told I had to write a book of poems that had to rhyme and be in specific forms or they wouldn't sell. When you worry about form that much, it is going to influence everything you do in a poem. Thank goodness how we view poetry has changed over the years.

JC: In the introduction to *Cold Stars and Fireflies,* you said you did the winter poems in summer, summer poems in winter. Do you think the collection would have been much different if you had done them "in season"?

BJE: No, because that season was in my head. You know, seasons have been in my head all of my life. I wrote the book in California because I think I was lonesome for the seasons. I went to the Eureka library every single day one summer and worked on those poems. I am a real procrastinator, so I had to schedule myself like that. The particular season didn't matter at all. I wrote what was in my head and what was interesting to me.

JC: Other than in a few poems, the reader doesn't get much information about the speakers of these pieces. Rather, the poems appear with a "neutral persona," which, in effect, lets the reader become the speaker. Is this why you use the neutral voice so much?

BJE: It doesn't need to be just "me" or "I" in poetry. It is good for children to know that all can or should have these experiences in life, and a neutral speaker will show that. I think it makes it easier for the children to say, "This is my world being described here." That's something I strive for in my work.

JC: One of your best-known poems, and my favorite in the *Cold Stars* collection, is "Fourth of July," the poem from which the title evolves. I think one line in that poem represents the best of Barbara Juster Esbensen: "We are fire worshippers." On one level in that line, we see average people enjoying fireworks. On another, we see people enjoying a use of fire in the way prehistoric people did. On still another, the reader can see the visual images, the reflection of the fire on those watching: fire worshippers. And the levels continue. How much editing and revising do you have to do on a conscious level to get the multiple meanings that appear so much in your work?

BJE: I don't do anything special to get these different levels. I think I always think of different levels at once. I was thinking of fire worshippers the way you are, about all these people with upturned faces watching this stuff happening, and I was also thinking that people looking at the volcano god would have had that same expression on their faces—you know, eons ago. That's what occurred to me. At first, I was just thinking of the crowd in Edina, Minnesota, and how they respond exactly the same primitive way that people did 20,000 years ago. At the time, it seemed to me that those were two things that would occur to everybody.

When I write some of the lines, they come to me so fast that I am surprised when somebody tells me that what I have done is different or out of the ordinary. I find that in conversation sometimes, too. I'll say something that I think we are all thinking, and everybody laughs and says my comments were funny, or different, or whatever. And I'm surprised by that. I guess I just see these things a little differently from some people.

JC: Your poetry has changed greatly since *Swing Around the Sun.* The poems in this collection were heavily rhymed. They were also more like still photographs in that each, like "Umbrellas," was focused on one central image as opposed to the natural linking of many images found in your newest work. What started this change in your style, and when did you free yourself from the rhyme?

BJE: Really, my style has not changed all that much. Remember, I was told I had to make the poems rhyme in order to get them sold. The rhyme was a result of comments from an editor. I had rarely rhymed poems before doing *Swing Around the Sun.* I remember thinking to myself that what would save these rhyming poems would be spectacular images. I felt that if I could work marvelous images into the poems and still have rhyme that I'd be okay. I did *not* want to end up with the "June-spoon-baboon" rhyming that I talk about in *A Celebration of Bees* (1975). I remember that I wanted the images to be so good that the reader didn't care if they rhymed or not. My favorite teacher, Miss Beffel, introduced me to the poetry of Sara Teasdale who often used rhyme, and the poetry of Amy Lowell who did not rhyme anything. I grew up with both types. So, while it looks like my style changed greatly after that book, it really didn't. And my next book, *Dance with Me*, has only rhymed poems, but I've hidden the rhyme in the middle of lines in many of them.

JC: How would you say your process of writing has changed through the years?

BJE: I don't have any real work habits as a poet. I mean, I do the same things I have always done. I give myself a list of things or possibilities I want to include in a book—either titles, topics, subjects, or pieces of ideas—and I look at a couple I think I can start on today. Then I take out a stack of fresh paper or mess around with the word processor and just start to work. I like to begin by dumping a lot of stuff out of my brain. For *Cold Stars and Fireflies* and *Swing Around the Sun,* I just thought first of all the things about seasons I remembered from my own childhood: making angels in the snow, skating on Lake Monona in Madison, Wisconsin, looking down through the ice and seeing seaweed even though I was way out in the middle of a lake. Those sorts of remembrances.

JC: Words with Wrinkled Knees (1986) is a very entertaining, very different sort of collection. What led to the creation of this book?

BJE: I think I have always thought about the image that a word becomes, the image that appears right after you say it. You and I can't say the word "horse" without picturing a horse. There are two horses in this room with us right now. When I go out to talk to children, I say to them, "Don't think about an elephant. I do *not* want you to think about an elephant. I hope you are *not* thinking about an elephant." Then I say to them that there are thirty-three elephants in the room right now and all are facing different ways and all look different. I thought I was going to write a book about words that *are* what they say. I thought it would have musical instrument words, weather words, animal words, and who knows what else. Animals were one of them, but animals weren't all I intended to do. I called my editor, Barbara Fenton, one day to see what she thought of this idea. I had written just three of the poems at that point, the ones about the elephant, hippopotamus, and xylophone. I read the animal poems over the phone to her, and she loved them. I then read the xylophone poem, and she said, "No, that's nice, but this is not going to be a book about words of all different kinds. This is going to be animal words." She loved the idea and told me to send other poems as I finished them.

It's funny, but that xylophone poem finally did get used. I added a top and bottom to it, and it is now in a collection of poems Myra Cohn Livingston gathered together for Holiday House. It is a spooky, ghostly poem now.

JC: The poems in *Words with Wrinkled Knees* have wonderful wordplay, especially in terms of arrangement and spacing of the words: the seahorse dangling down the page, the letters in the centipede poem spaced to represent length, "lion" spaced to show open jaws.

BJE: I didn't want to do too much of that. I didn't think spacing here was as important as getting the right sorts of images in the poems. But there are a few more examples here. In the owl poem I spaced out not the owl but the *sailing* into the dark. I wanted that word to go out to represent the action within the poem. I wanted it to give a movement to the brain. In the camel poem, the *M* provides the humps to store the water. At times, the spacing itself can provide beautiful images, images that will touch the reader.

JC: The poems in this collection are very unusual, very striking. Which is your favorite?

BJE: The poem about the wolf is my favorite. The book didn't have a title for about a year. I had been pulling lines out of poems trying to find a line that really captured the whole collection. I drew a line from this wolf poem and sent it to my editor. After she read it, she told me the poem was not clear to her. It was incomplete in some way. I kept picturing this wolf over and over, and I was picturing snow with the wolf, and I hadn't said anything in the poem about snow! Then I added the snow and the whole poem fell into place. I didn't use a line from the poem for the title, but I loved the poem after the changes. It was just one of those experiences where everything fell into place in a poem, but not until after a lot of hard work.

JC: *A Celebration of Bees* is a book many teachers have read and used when helping young children write poetry. In the introduction to this book, you say the poet wants to use our ordinary, everyday language in new ways to make that language open new doors and let us see the world in ways we haven't noticed before. You also say that poetry is a capturing of essences, and words are the traps you set to do the job. Which traps do you hope your readers fall into? What is it you hope your readers do while reading?

BJE: I want them to make a connection between themselves and me. Good poetry ought to be able to do that so that they say, "Oh yeah—yeah, that's just right." When I read to children, I tell them to keep their hands down the first time. Then I tell them I'm going to read the poem again, and this time I want them to raise their hands every time they hear a lie or something that can't possibly be happening in the real world. During the second reading, hands go up all the time. That's what I want the readers to be able to do. I want them to know when something is exactly right and be able to realize when something isn't really, really right. It could be just emotionally right, right in terms of imagery, or psychologically right.

JC: In *A Celebration of Bees* you also say that children should forget about rhyme at first when writing poetry because it can force meaningless poems. Isn't that quite difficult to get across to them?

BJE: Not only forget about rhyme at first, but forget about rhyme forever. I tell them that I have written some poems that rhyme, and I can do that because of years of working with the language. I think about the images first and the rhyme only incidentally. With rhyme you always have a sense of what's coming at the end of the line, and that ruins the surprise. To me, poetry should knock your block off. Rhyme most of the time interferes with that. I tell them just to say what they want to say. I tell them nothing has to rhyme, and their brains are full of wonderful images that are going to turn rotten if they try to force them into something called rhyme. Words get rammed into spaces that they just don't want to be in.

JC: In this book you express a three-part philosophy: When working with young poets, one must demonstrate acceptance, respect, and understanding. As a part of this, the guide *must* look for and find something of real or potential value in each effort. Please elaborate upon these ideas.

BJE: I can find something positive in each attempt. I might say something like, "I can see that you are trying to write about your shoe, but right now I don't see a difference between your shoes and mine. What are your shoes thinking? Let's get inside your shoes. Does your shoe have a way of talking? Who or what would it talk with? After all, it has a tongue! Maybe there's another shoe that is only a sandal. That shoe doesn't have a tongue. How does the first shoe feel about the second?" And so on and so on and so on.

JC: You do this so well with children because of your experience. How about for beginning teachers?

BJE: I think teachers have to be writers themselves. I always suggest that teachers get into some sort of writing group. That can be a great experience because it teaches them once again about the creative process. They remember the agony they go through in coming up with ideas, and that helps them recognize that even the effort a child puts into this is very important. I always think of this analogy: You wouldn't try to teach children how to read music if you'd never read music.

JC: Do you have a special message you would like to send along to your readers?

BJE: What I would like people to look for in my writing, or any other person's writing for that matter, is a fresh look at what everybody sees all the time. We all have the same feelings, basically. We all live in the same kinds of bodies. We all live on the same planet. In order to express how we feel about where we are, who we are, and what we see, we need to think of new ways of expressing ourselves. That "new expression" is what I hope to provide always for my readers.

Select Bibliography

Echoes for the Eye: More Poems of Discovery (HarperCollins, forthcoming).

Dance with Me (HarperCollins, forthcoming).

Who Shrank My Grandmother's House: Poems of Discovery (HarperCollins, 1992).

Words with Wrinkled Knees (Harper & Row, 1986).

Cold Stars and Fireflies (Harper & Row, 1984).
Swing Around the Sun (Lerner Publications, 1965).

Books about Poetry

A Celebration of Bees: Helping Children Write Poetry (Harper & Row, 1975).

William Cole

William Cole's career as a writer has been shaped by stints as an editor, freelance writer, and bookstore manager. Today, he is a poet who also happens to assemble anthologies for children and young adults; these volumes have grown to number over fifty. He has devoted much of his life to making poetry accessible to the young through these anthologies.

Cole describes himself as something of a "pack rat" because of the clutter produced from having nearly four thousand volumes of poetry stacked in his home. From these volumes, and from volumes found in public and private libraries, Cole has compiled some of the most popular modern collections of verse: Oh, Such Foolishness *(1991),* Poem Stew *(1981),* Dinosaurs and Beasts of Yore *(1979),* An Arkful of Animals *(1978), and* Beastly Boys and Ghastly Girls *(1964).*

His own poetry is characterized by strong rhythm and rhyme. Cole likes to select a subject and then "rhyme it all up." He views poetry as a puzzle that should both entertain and enlighten young readers.

Today, William Cole writes poetry and assembles anthologies in New York City.

JC: The first poetry anthology you designed for children was *Humorous Poetry for Children* (1955). How did the process of putting that book together then compare to and differ from the process you now use to assemble an anthology? In other words, how have you grown, both naturally and from necessity, as an anthologist?

WC: It used to be scissors and paste. The biggest change for me, honestly, has been the availability of photocopy machines. I used to clip poems out of books and then throw the books away. Honestly. I have a good library now—about five hundred books of children's poetry and about four thousand other books of poetry. I have these right here in my own home, so access to the material is easy. If I need a particular poem, chances are excellent it is waiting for me right in my own library.

Photo: Elliott Erwitt © 1963 Magnum Photos

JC: What is the rubric you employ when selecting poems for a volume? To you, what makes a good poem?

WC: First and foremost, I look for something vivid. I look for poems that have "surprise." I want poems that will tell us something different about a subject.

The book that best represents me and the process I go through is *Poems from Ireland* (1972); it is a fine book. It is now out of print, but I dearly love that book and loved doing it. I'm very Irish myself, so I really cared about the material that went into it. I also got into that book everybody I wanted to get in. The publisher did, however, cut me back some because it just simply got too big. Editors do that on occasion.

JC: If you were given an unlimited budget to cover permission fees and could do any type of collection you wanted to do, what would you create?

WC: I would do a big one, a huge one. I'd call it *Surprise and Joy!* I'd include all the poems that I really love and that I feel would be most appropriate for children. I'd include all subjects in the volume—everything a young reader could be excited by. I'd also like to do another short, short collection for kids. I did one called *Pick Me Up: A Book of Short Poems* (1972). I love that collection. There is so much in the way of good poetry around for kids that there is room for another good short book.

JC: What do you see as the future of the anthology?

WC: I don't think the future looks too good for the anthology because of permission fees. Publishers are now asking an awful lot of money for a poem—anywhere from fifty dollars to a thousand for a single poem! That makes it very difficult for the publisher and anthologist to profit from the project. And money, of course, is the bottom line in the business world. The only people doing much in the way of anthologies would be Lee Bennett Hopkins, Paul Janeczko, Dorothy and X.J. Kennedy, and me, really. Jack Prelutsky and Myra Cohn Livingston also do some, but not as much because of their other interests and talents.

JC: From your vantage point as one of the people most knowledgeable about contemporary children's poetry, please recommend for children a volume of poetry they might not know about but you find to be an extra-special collection. At the same time, please suggest a specific poet for the young readers to examine.

WC: There is a new version of *The Golden Journey*, the collection William Jay Smith did with Louise Bogan. He has expanded the book and made it much more attractive. It is quite simply a wonderful book for children. It is mostly a collection of lyrical poetry that will touch them. I am also especially fond of another of Smith's books, *A Green Place*. That was published in 1982. It was just Smith by himself. He is very good as a light verse poet. Younger children find his work fascinating, and I wish more would discover his work.

In my opinion, the most underrated poet in the world is Spike Milligan, the Irish poet. It is simply ridiculous that he has never had a whole book of poetry published over here. He has published over ten books in England. His poetry is universal; humor and surprise play the same in all parts of the world. I hope he gets published here so that American children get to see just how good he really is. Spike Milligan is so funny! He is a movie actor, theater performer, comedian. As it is now, children get only glimpses of his work in anthologies. Of course, that is one of the primary purposes of the anthology: to introduce new poets to new generations of readers.

If a child is eight or older, I would suggest giving him or her e. e. cummings's collected poems. They would make a wonderful bridge between concerns of childhood and concerns of the more mature. I would also recommend Robert Frost for children who are a little older. Frost will definitely introduce them to a new world.

JC: You have said on many occasions that you know little of the definitions and traditional elements of poetry, yet your own poems are superbly designed, especially in terms of rhythm and meter. How do you account for this seeming paradox?

WC: I guess I just have a very good idea. What I do is take an idea and rhyme it all up. For me, it is like doing a puzzle. I sit there, and the meter comes naturally. I know it's not always perfect. The rhymes are the most fun for me to do. I'll even admit now that once in a while I use a rhyming dictionary. Why not? I have done a few poems for adults that don't rhyme, but generally I'm a light verse poet who has to have rhyme and meter carry the poem. This is also a good message for younger children who wish to write poetry. Go ahead and write it; go ahead and have fun with the language. When you get interested later you can sit back and learn the terms and background. Have fun first!

JC: Tell us about the major influences upon you as a writer.

WC: When I was a youngster, I was involved with collecting stamps and sneaking into movie theaters. I really was like the brats I have written about. I had done some writing in high school, but not very much. However, my life really changed when I went into the service. Looking back, I can say that that was the most important thing that ever happened to me, both personally and for my writing. I started a regimental newspaper called the *Old Gray Mare*, and writing for this transformed me as a writer. I wrote editorials, reports, a little humor, and pieces about popular humorists of the day. This was very much a growth experience for me. When I came back to New York after the war, I worked in publishing and excelled at writing news releases. Finally, my first poem was published in the *New Yorker*; it was called "Just Dropped In." From there, my career took off.

JC: When you write poetry, what process of composing do you employ?

WC: Often when I'm in bed in the morning I get an idea for a poem. Then, I go through the alphabet to see what words there are that seem to fit with my original idea. I think of things like what word rhymes with others and start to shape poems in my head this way. One day when I was in bed I was thinking of the most absurd situations I could come up with and came to the idea for my favorite of my poems, "A Boy Named Mary Jane" (from *A Boy Named Mary Jane, and Other Silly Verse*, 1977). I am a light-verse poet, an aficionado of light verse. I look at light poems as puzzles for children. I want them to have fun playing with these puzzles.

JC: In your early anthologies you wrote prose introductions, and none of your own poems appeared in the collections. Through the years, however, you started writing "introduction poems" to set the tone for the collections and began including many more of your own poems in the books. Was this conscious or just a natural evolution for the anthologist?

WC: It has mostly been a natural progression. *An Arkful of Animals* has a very short introduction poem to set the tone. For that one I had written a very long poem, but an editor at the publishing company cut it down to what you now see in the book. I really liked the longer version, but editors do those things. I love writing poems as introductions. They are advertisements, really. One of my newest books is *A Zooful of Animals* (1992). I liked the sound of that "zooful" word. It also has a short introductory verse. In terms of my own poetry, I really didn't write that much until I saw what fun it was. Then I started putting my own poems in the collections. After all, who else would publish them?

JC: The Birds and the Beasts Were There (1963) is representative of your work as an anthologist. Much of your work is about animals and our coexistence with them. In that collection the reader finds a large number of poems that deal with cruelty to animals. Did you include that group of poems to present a personal message?

WC: I detest cruelty to animals. That was a personal message. That is an area that is close to my heart. In that collection, just as important to me as the quality of the poems was that message to all people. In terms of this subject, I'd like to add a two-line poem that has never been in a book. I call it "A Blakeian Couplet." It goes like this:

> The distinction between man and animal blurs
> When he clothes himself in animal furs.

I'd like to give that as a slogan to one of the groups protecting the rights and dignity of animals.

JC: A story that has become legend in children's poetry has to do with the origin of *Beastly Boys and Ghastly Girls.* How much of that story is true and how much legend?

WC: It's all true. I was having a wonderful conversation about subjects for anthologies with an editor from Dial Press. This particular editor was from the Deep South and had a very pronounced drawl. I could have sworn she suggested I do a book about "brat" children, so that's what I did: I went off and put together a volume about brats. What she really said was that I should put together a collection for "bright" kids. It was her drawl that led me to the other. It is funny, however, because the volume has been one of my bestsellers.

JC: Do you have a special message for readers of your work?

WC: Read and look for things that you care about. Be enthusiastic in your reading and in all aspects of your life. Be creative. Use writing to create beauty in the world.

If I can get some kids reading poetry, then life will have been worthwhile for me.

Select Bibliography

Anthologies Edited

A Zooful of Animals (Houghton Mifflin, 1992).

Oh, Such Foolishness (HarperCollins, revised edition, 1991).

Oh, That's Ridiculous! (Puffin Books, revised edition, 1988).

Good Dog Poems (Scribner, 1981).

Poem Stew (J. B. Lippincott, 1981).

Dinosaurs and Beasts of Yore (HarperCollins, 1979).

The Poetry of Horses (Scribner, 1979).

An Arkful of Animals (Houghton Mifflin, 1978).

I'm Mad at You (HarperCollins, 1978).

A Boy Named Mary Jane, and Other Silly Verse (Franklin Watts, 1977).

A Book of Animal Poems (Viking, 1973).

Pick Me Up: A Book of Short Poems (Macmillan, 1972).

Poems from Ireland (Thomas Y. Crowell, 1972).

Oh, How Silly! (Viking, 1971).

The Book of Giggles (World Publishing, 1970).

A Book of Nature Poems (Viking, 1969).

Oh, What Nonsense! (Viking, 1966).

Beastly Boys and Ghastly Girls (World Publishing, 1964).

The Birds and the Beasts Were There (World Publishing, 1963).

Humorous Poetry for Children (World Publishing, 1955).

Eve Merriam

Eve Merriam relished her role as the grand dame of children's poetry. Through a lifetime of speeches, sharing sessions, and workshops in the schools, she introduced thousands of teachers and children to the delights of poetry. She called these sessions her greatest joy in life.

Merriam believed that children should be introduced to poetry first through light, humorous verse. She gave this poetry to young readers in such collections as Chortles: New and Selected Wordplay Poems *(1989) and* Jamboree: Rhymes for All Times *(1984). She was a punster who found great joy in the sounds and unusual combinations of words. Her poetry for young children was characterized by this playful and skillful use of language, and in 1981 she was awarded the National Council of Teachers of English Award for Excellence in Poetry for Children. Eve Merriam was also a champion of women's rights who fought to eliminate sex-role stereotyping from children's literature. In her poetry, the world is seen as a place where all possibilities exist for all people.*

Eve Merriam passed away shortly after granting the following interview. She leaves behind a legacy of love for life and for poetry.

JC: The typical speaker found within your poems is a young, inquisitive, full-of-joy human being. This speaker is also not designated as male or female; rather, the speaker is a human being first, a member of the world. And, this is a nonsexist world.

EM: I have been a feminist all of my life. I believe first and foremost in equality of the sexes, equality of everybody on earth. I am particularly involved in trying to do nonsexist work in literature for the young. I'm very conscious, for example, of not using "he" all the time in my writings. As a matter of fact, when I first started writing poetry for children, I wrote an essay, and in it I referred to the poet as "he." It has been reissued in an issue of *Writer* magazine, and I revised it so that instead of saying "he" I just said "the poet." Also, when I wrote "Millie

Photo: Bachrach

and Willie" (from *There Is No Rhyme for Silver,* 1962) I wanted to show that boys can be dumb and silly and girls can be dumb and silly—that we are all equal in every single way. I once did a tape for the National Education Association called "Blue Is for Sky and Pink Is for Watermelon." In this I did a number of my nonsexist poems on cassette.

JC: Another hallmark of your poetry is masterful blending of wordplay and sounds. A volume that is especially representative of this is *Chortles,* which brings together many of your best and most requested poems. Is this blend an outgrowth of your belief that poetry should be read aloud for greatest enjoyment?

EM: I love to fool around with language. The language, really, is like a game. Some people like to bounce balls or jump rope, and I like to skip around and doodle with the sounds of words. Children do, too. I remember that when my own sons were very little, we had sycamore trees on our street. They used to say the word "sycamore, sycamore" over and over again and thought that was so funny. I also remember once using the word "encyclopedia," and they heard it and went into gales of laughter. I realized that if you looked at the word on the printed page you wouldn't get the joke, but saying the word slowly and aloud almost put them into convulsions.

One of the great differences between prose and poetry is that poetry has its own built-in music. Who would think of listening to music by just looking at a score on a page? You have to hear the poem aloud to get the alliteration, the resonance, the assonance, the repetition, all the wonderful vowel sounds that open up, the consonance that sort of clusters. That's my great joy: to turn people on to the delight in the sounds of syllables and words.

JC: A reader of your poetry cannot be lazy. Because of these rhythms and sounds, the reader must be actively involved in the lines by clapping or moving or singing.

EM: Particularly with children, but even with kids in the upper-elementary grades, I like to get children involved in the lines. I have a new collection coming out in the fall of 1992 which will be called *The Singing Green: New and Selected Poems for Young Readers.* I purposely wrote some new poems for this that were like rap songs that have terrific rhythm to them. When you read them you really have to move with the lines to get the greatest enjoyment. I have one in that collection called "Travelling" that is about places you can go, different cities to visit. It has lines like, "Spend a coin/In Des Moines," "Go to a disco/In San Francisco." The whole collection is really put together to get people moving with the language. That is what poetry is all about. That is what I'm all about.

I also have a poem called "Umbilical" (from *A Sky Full of Poems,* 1986) that has been used a lot. I remember once going to a junior high school in an inner city, and there were a lot of big, tough boys. I just knew they were thinking, "Oh gosh, here comes this old lady walking in and she's going to give us very pretty, little stuff." I started right away snapping my fingers, and I began chanting with the best rhythm I could muster, "You can take away my mother/You can take away my sister/But don't take away/My little transistor." Their ears started to perk up, and a universal language was found. I like to give people the fun and true pleasure of sounds.

I also used to do some tap dancing when I was young, and I think this is a big reason why I like to get movement into the lines. I think rather than having people of any age, whether it is nursery school or kindergarten or on up, just sitting passively, if you can get them involved this will help develop a love and appreciation for poetry. Sometimes when I do a reading, I will do a line and then have them repeat it. Or if there is a chorus, we will all clap our hands or snap our fingers or tap our feet. I get them to do what I call "taking a poetry breath." This is inhaling, letting the breath out very slowly, and then shaking their fingers—to show them that you need to use all five senses to be aware of language. I think the most important thing of all is that young people get an appreciation for poetry.

JC: What suggestions do you have for teachers, librarians, and others who are attempting to develop this appreciation?

EM: Read it aloud! Read it aloud! Read it aloud! Sample all different kinds of poetry with the children. Make poetry a smorgasbord. Read a serious poem. Read a light poem. Read things on different topics. Keep on sharing poetry in this fashion until there is something all of the kids like and can start finding on their own.

Personally, when I read I try to give a little background to the poem. When I do the poem "Portmanteau" (from *A Word or Two with You: New Rhymes for Young Readers,* 1981), I put it on the blackboard and explain the derivation of the word, that it is a combination of words, and that it comes from the French and is a cloak which is embracing all these things. I'll say that sometimes on the weekends, if you sleep late or your parents sleep late, you might have a meal that is served late in the morning. What would that be called? Of course somebody will say "brunch." I'll say that that is a "portmanteau" word, a combination of the words *breakfast* and *lunch*. If you are out and the sky looks very dark yet it is not raining, what do you think there might be in the air? Somebody usually says "smog." Then I read the poem "Portmanteau." I try as much as possible when I am in the classroom to give them something visual, something to look at, as well as my being there and getting them to use their bodies when they experience poetry. So, if there is a word or title I can put on the blackboard or a phrase for them to read out loud, then I do that. I really feel that helps set the right tone and atmosphere.

I also believe in getting them to repeat things or read with me. I'll divide them into groups and tell some to do one part of the poem and others to do other sections or verses. Then I'll say, "Let's see how fast we can do this poem!" I never want to leave the classroom with the students all hyped up, so I then ask them to see how slowly they can read the poem. In these ways I try to gain control over the moods. With young children particularly, at least every five minutes I ask them to sit up straight and take deep poetry breaths or stretch necks way up like a giraffe. All of this makes poetry fun, enjoyable for the children. After all, this is what poetry is all about.

It pleases me a lot when young children who normally can't sit still for more than five minutes are as good as can be for long periods of time while we share poetry. Once I was in a school where there was an autistic child who the teacher said had never done anything in the classroom. This child came up to me after our session and talked to me and gave me a little treasure of a dinosaur key ring. His teacher said that responding to the poetry was the first time he had responded to anything. Those are memories I will treasure forever.

I have also done a number of poems I call jump-rope poems or skip-rope rhymes. Once I was in a school reading to the children, and the gym teacher said she did not want to be left out of the activities. She literally got the students to jump rope while we read the rhymes. The children loved it! I want children most of all to have fun with poetry. And when reading poetry, children should be encouraged to read the poems at least twice: once to get the sense, and the second to get the music.

JC: Your poetry contains a great deal of humor. As a matter of fact, most of your poems are downright funny, and children laugh and giggle while reading them.

EM: I have always been a punster, have been all of my life. I write poetry for adults, too, and have always had a lot of puns in that work.

This is the case in my whole family. My two sons are wonderful punsters, and we always have a great deal of fun kidding around with the language. It's something that comes naturally in my family. I like to look at the absurdity of things. I also think there are just funny sounds and funny things that occur in life. Writing about these comes in a natural way to me. I also like humorous material myself. For example, in *Chortles* there is "By the Shores of Pago Pago." That is a perfect poem to illustrate how you really have to read poems out loud for true enjoyment. Yes, you can get words like "Mimi's dancing in a muumuu" and "Fifi is in a tutu." However, if you look at the word *cookoo* on the page, the syllables don't repeat exactly. But, when you say them aloud, they do. It would never occur to me that children would not like funny things.

Another of my poems I like to share with children is "Rover" (from *A Word or Two with You*). I took this from an old shaggy dog joke that was making the rounds. I find funny things everywhere; that's the kind of person I am. I don't think I can sit down and say, "Hey, I want to write a funny poem." It comes naturally to me because I see things as funny.

JC: When you read the works of others, do you also search for this humor to provide an enjoyable reading experience for yourself? Tell us about Eve Merriam, the poetry reader.

EM: When I read a poem and can share in the feelings of the lines, whether they be sad or terrible feelings or happy feelings or being in love, and the poem speaks to me directly without any intermediary, to me that is a beautiful poem. For me, it is usually the content of a poem or the way something is phrased that touches me. One of my favorite poets in the world is Gerard Manley Hopkins, the Jesuit poet. When I was in college and first read his poetry, my skin just prickled, and I knew these were verses I had to hold onto all my life. I still have a poster in my bedroom of one of his poems. There was something about the way in which he phrased words to make them so dense and packed. W. H. Auden was one of my teachers. He had such a gift for wit and precision in use of the language. I know that rubbed off on me. I also loved reading Yeats and T. S. Eliot. They all have in their poetry phrases that touch my soul. I want today's children to find poets who touch them. I want them to be able to say, "I'm not alone in the world. Somebody else has the same feelings I have." When a child says to me, "Gee, I never wanted to read poetry, but your stuff is kind of fun," I just feel that makes life worth living for me.

JC: Do you think too much is done with young children in terms of explication of poetry, in formal study of the terms of poetry, and the like?

EM: Absolutely! I came across a poem of mine used in a textbook, and it had several study questions with it. I'm telling you the truth when I say I couldn't answer the questions that went with that poem. There is also a poem I wrote called "Cheers" (from *It Doesn't Always Have to Rhyme*, 1964), which I have seen in textbooks. It is simply playing around with the language, and in it the frogs and the serpents each have a football team. I used plosives for the frogs, sibilants for the serpents, and had a great time playing with words. A question I saw that went with it asked why the poet used certain words and what they meant. Well, the truth of the matter is I used the words because it was fun for me to play around with the words and their sounds. There wasn't anything deeper than that, although children would think otherwise if they believed the questions. Poetry too often becomes intimidating because of the study that goes with it. People should lighten up, should enjoy the language first and foremost.

I tell people, I don't care what synecdoche is. Forget the terms. I don't care if a poem is iambic or anapestic or whatever. Do the beats naturally and think about what it means to you, read the language aloud, and get pleasure out of it. Otherwise, poetry will be intimidating not just for the children but for the teachers as well. I am very glad to see the whole-language programs that are popping up around the country, because in these we are emphasizing reading and the joyousness of it without all of this dusty stuff.

If there has to be some sort of formal study of poetry, I'd like to see people do what I have done and enjoyed a great deal. I ask the students to bring in two poems they like very much and two that they dislike. When I have readers do this, someone will bring in a poem and say he or she didn't understand it. Then we'll read it and either find something in it together or I'll say, "You know, I don't think it is so hot either. We don't have to read that again. We'll move on to another one." With poems they like, we'll talk about what in the poems gave them pleasure, why the poems touched them the way they did. We'll talk about what in their own lives we saw in the poems.

There are plenty of paperback anthologies and other sources of poems available. Those who share poetry with the young should have stacks of these available. I once met a librarian who said, "I'm a poetry guerrilla. I run into classes for two minutes, read a poem, and run out again." She did this just to keep poetry in front of the students and a regular part of the school activities. Teachers can and should do this too. Poetry is so brief and condensed that it can be used in any situation.

Sometimes when I go visit schools, before the school day begins they will read one of my poems over the loudspeaker when the early morning announcements are given. I say to them, "That was nice, but why not do this all year round!" I have also used poems in mathematics classes, social science classes, physical education programs—all sorts of places in the school. This pleases me greatly. We can and should weave poems into all areas. Poetry must be fun!

Select Bibliography

The Singing Green: New and Selected Poems for Young Readers (Morrow Jr. Books, 1992).

Chortles: New and Selected Wordplay Poems (Morrow Jr. Books, 1989).

A Poem for a Pickle: Funnybone Verses (Morrow Jr. Books, 1989).

You Be Good & I'll Be Night: Jump-on-the-Bed Poems (Morrow Jr. Books, 1988).

Halloween ABC (Macmillan, 1987).

Fresh Paint (Macmillan, 1986).

A Sky Full of Poems (Dell, 1986).

Blackberry Ink (Morrow Jr. Books, 1985).

Jamboree: Rhymes for All Times (Dell, 1984).

If Only I Could Tell You: Poems for Young Lovers and Daydreamers (Alfred A. Knopf, 1983).

A Word or Two with You: New Rhymes for Young Readers (Atheneum, 1981).

Rainbow Writing (Atheneum, 1976).

Out Loud (Atheneum, 1973).

Finding a Poem (Atheneum, 1970).

Independent Voices (Atheneum, 1968).

Catch a Little Rhyme (Atheneum, 1966).

It Doesn't Always Have to Rhyme (Atheneum, 1964).

There Is No Rhyme for Silver (Atheneum, 1962).

Editor

Photo: Vicky L. Copeland

Jeffrey S. Copeland is associate professor of English education at the University of Northern Iowa where he teaches children's and young adult literature courses, composition courses, and a variety of English education methods courses. Copeland's first love in literature is poetry written for children and young adults, and he has written/edited seven poetry texts, including *Hiccups and Giggles* (1985), *The Shooting Star: A Poetry Anthology* (1985), and *Ogres and Ugstabuggles* (1991). He lives today with his wife, Vicky, and his daughter, Crystal Lynn, in Cedar Falls, Iowa.